*UNDERSTANDING*

# EQUINE
# COLIC

YOUR **GUIDE** TO HORSE HEALTH
CARE AND MANAGEMENT

ISBN 1-58150-112-9


Printed in the United States of America
First Edition: March 2004
1 2 3 4 5 6 7 8 9 10

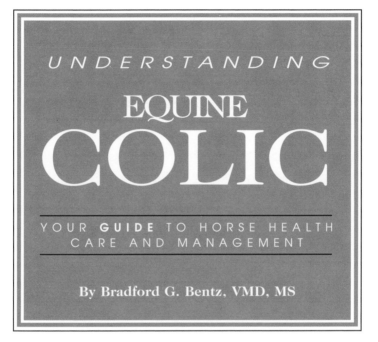

*UNDERSTANDING*

## EQUINE
# COLIC

YOUR **GUIDE** TO HORSE HEALTH
CARE AND MANAGEMENT

By Bradford G. Bentz, VMD, MS

Blood-Horse Publications, Lexington, KY

Other titles offered by
*The Horse* Health Care Library

*Understanding* Equine Acupuncture

*Understanding* Basic Horse Care

*Understanding* Breeding Management

*Understanding* the Broodmare

*Understanding* Equine Business Basics

*Understanding* the Equine Eye

*Understanding* Equine First Aid

*Understanding* the Foal

*Understanding* the Equine Foot

*Understanding* Horse Behavior

*Understanding* Laminitis

*Understanding* Equine Lameness

*Understanding* Equine Law

*Understanding* Equine Medications

*Understanding* Equine Neurological Disorders

*Understanding* Equine Nutrition

*Understanding* the Older Horse

*Understanding* the Pony

*Understanding* Equine Preventive Medicine

*Understanding* EPM

*Understanding* the Stallion

*Understanding* the Young Horse

# Contents

## INTRODUCTION

# Why the Horse Is Prone to Colic

An equine surgeon friend once said "the person who designed the equine intestinal tract must have worked on it all day Saturday and taken Sunday off." His statement is humorous but true. The overall "design" of the equine intestinal system is fraught with problems that make it highly susceptible to permitting intestine to move into places where it should not be and out of places where it is supposed to remain. Thereafter, it often gets distended and subsequently cannot return to its correct location. Although this is certainly an overgeneralization of equine colic episodes, the high occurrence of colic and the need for abdominal surgery (colic surgery) in the horse are much higher than in nearly any other species; thus, my surgeon friend's reference to the flaw in the engineering and subsequent design of the equine intestinal tract.

In the following pages we will explain more fully the occurrence of "intestinal accidents" and other causes of many types of colic (abdominal pain) that are recognized in the horse. To explain these conditions, it will be necessary to understand some of the basic anatomy and physiology of the equine intestinal tract. We will also introduce many terms that are explained in the text and in the accompanying glossary.

## ANATOMY OF THE EQUINE INTESTINAL TRACT AND ABDOMEN

In a very broad sense the equine intestinal tract can be divided into large sections based on its overall function. These sections are analogous to the same segments that exist in most mammals. They include the stomach, small intestine, the large intestine, and the small colon. The stomach is a large sac that liquefies the feed that is ingested by the horse. Only a small amount of digestion occurs in the stomach. No nu-

> # AT A GLANCE
>
> • A herbivore, the horse is designed to graze.
>
> • Domestication of the horse is at odds with the natural design of its intestinal system.
>
> • The design of the horse's intestinal tract makes the animal prone to problems such as colic.

trients are absorbed through the stomach. Acid from the stomach helps to break down some feed particles, and an enzyme known as pepsin begins protein digestion. True digestion only begins in the small intestine that receives this liquefied feed material from the stomach. With assistance from the enzymes secreted by the pancreas into the small intestine, the small intestine is the primary site for digestion and absorption of sugar and starch (a complex sugar in plants), protein (that

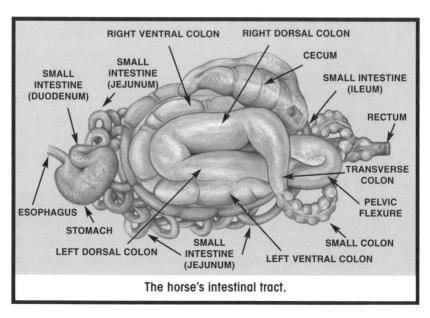

The horse's intestinal tract.

has been initially digested in the stomach), and fat. The small intestine is also the site for absorption of fat-soluble vitamins (A, D, E, and K), calcium, and phosphorous.

The next segment, the large intestine, begins with the cecum and ends with the descending colon. The large intestine in the horse works like a large fermentation vat in which tremendous numbers of bacteria and protozoa live to facilitate further digestion of plant fiber by their production of enzymes that are capable of breaking down this component of the equine diet (the horse itself does not have these enzymes). This fiber breakdown produces substances called "volatile fatty acids" that can then be absorbed and used by the horse for energy. A second important function of the large intestine is water absorption. This function occurs very efficiently such that by the final step in the small colon, the waste material not used by the horse is formed into fecal balls. These are subsequently passed into the rectum for evacuation through the anus.

As a herbivore the horse is "designed" to graze and, therefore, must be equipped with a capacity to extract nutrition from grass and other forage. This process requires an area of the intestinal tract where the forage can ferment to release absorbable and usable forms of energy (the volatile fatty acids). The horse, a "hindgut" fermenter, differs from "foregut" fermenters such as ruminants (cattle, sheep, goats). In horses fermentation occurs primarily in specialized areas of the lower intestinal tract: the cecum and large intestine. Ruminants perform this fermentation in the rumen, the largest compartment of a four-chambered stomach "system."

The horse's intestinal tract begins with the mouth and esophagus. The esophagus of the adult horse is approximately 1 1/4 to 1 1/2 meters in length. As in humans, it serves to pass food and water to the stomach through muscular contractions of the esophageal wall. The esophagus opens into the stomach at the esophageal sphincter.

The size of the equine stomach, a "j-shaped" organ, varies

but generally holds between 8 and 15 liters, depending partly on the size of the horse. Two distinctly different types of mucosa (intestinal lining) exist within the stomach. One is continuous with the esophageal sphincter. This mucosa is termed the "non-glandular" and "squamous" portion because it does not have any stomach glands that secrete acid, mucus, or digestive enzymes. This "non-glandular" portion of the stomach extends about halfway into the stomach where it meets the second type of stomach lining called the "glandular" portion of the stomach. When someone is looking in the stomach with an endoscope, this junction, called the margo plicatus, is seen as a distinct line midway into the stomach. From this junction the glandular portion of the stomach extends to the pylorus. The "glandular" harbors the glands that produce and release stomach acid and the protein-digesting enzyme pepsin. The pylorus of the stomach is the very farthest portion of the stomach from the mouth. It terminates in a muscular sphincter, the pyloric sphincter, which leads into the first portion of the small intestine.

The small intestine is generally about 22 meters (60-65 feet) long. It is composed of three distinct sections. The duodenum is the first segment and is only about a meter long. At about 12 to 15 centimeters from the pyloric sphincter, the pancreatic duct and bile duct empty into the duodenum (just beyond the location of the pyloric sphincter). The next and largest segment of the small intestine is the jejunum. It is highly mobile and exists in several coils primarily within the top portion (toward the spine) of the left half of the abdomen. The last part of the small intestine is about a meter long and is called the ileum. The small intestine does not hold any significant volume since the feedstuff travels through relatively quickly. If it is "holding" feed, it is probably abnormal.

The mesentery (ligamentous attachment of the intestine to the body wall) is connected to the top of the abdomen (toward the spine) near the first and second lumbar vertebrae at the site known as the "root of the mesentery." Within the root of the mesentery exists the large cranial mesenteric artery. The mesentery is wide and fan-shaped and carries numerous vessels and nerves to the intestines. It is attached to the small intestine along its entire length, but because of its fan shape and singular attachment, it is highly mobile and permits the small intestine to move freely in the abdomen. Embedded within the mesentery are lymph nodes and fat.

From the ileum (last part of the small intestine) arises the large structure known as the cecum, which is comma shaped and averages about 1 1/4 meters in length with a potential volume of 20 liters or more. Ruminants and even people have a cecum (in the human it is the appendix). However, the function and size are greatly expanded in the horse. The cecum, in horses, is a large, blunt-ended structure that forms sort of a T with the small intestine (the ileum) and large intestine (large colon). The cecum is the stem of the T, and the small and large intestine connect to it but not to each other.

There are two different entrances to the cecum, one from the small intestine and one from the colon. The cecum is blind ended and extends away from the "connections" (orifaces) to the small intestine and large colon. The entrance of the ileum into the cecum is termed the ileocecal orifice (one branch of the "top" of the "T") and about 5 centimeters from the entrance of the ileum into the cecum is the exit of the large colon from the cecum, the cecocolic orifice (the second branch of the top of the "T"). Normally, the ileum exists on the "underside" (or belly) of the horse. The apex or tip of the cecum lies on the abdominal floor just to the right of midline and about a hand's length back from the tip of the horse's sternum.

As its name implies, the large intestine is larger than the other parts of the intestinal tract. The large intestine, from the termination of the ileum to the anus of the horse, is about 7.5 to 8 meters in length. The terms "large intestine" and "large colon" are often used interchangeably. However, the large colon begins at the cecocolic orifice and extends about 3 to 3.7 meters to the transverse colon. The large colon exists in various diameters. About 5 to 7.5 centimeters in diameter near the cecocolic orifice, it expands to 20 to 25 centimeters on the floor of the abdomen and reaches a diameter of approximately 8 centimeters at the pelvic flexure, or turn. After this flexure it travels forward toward the head where it turns again at the diaphragmatic flexure and expands to nearly 50 centimeters in diameter. This segment is followed by the next section of large intestine, the transverse colon. The large intestine can really be described as the cecum, the large colon, the transverse colon, and small colon.

As already suggested, the entire intestinal system cannot exist within the abdomen in full extension. Therefore, it must be folded on itself to fit. The major abdominal turns in the horse are the sternal flexure, where the right ventral (on the floor of the abdomen) colon changes direction and turns left toward the tail. Then the left ventral colon changes direction and passes back toward the tail from the sternal flexure to turn dorsally (toward the spine) at the pelvic flexure. From there the left dorsal colon (on top of the ventral colon nearer to the spine) courses back toward the head of the diaphragm, turns right at the diaphragmatic flexure (situated above the sternal flexure), and gives rise to the right dorsal colon (on top of the right ventral colon nearer to the spine). The right dorsal colon then courses back again toward the tail and turns left toward the middle of the abdomen to become the shorter and narrower transverse colon. The transverse colon joins the small colon just below the left kidney. The small colon is about 3.5 meters in length and begins at the termination of the shorter transverse colon. Small colon diameter ranges from 7.5 to 10 centimeters. The small colon is followed by the final segment, the rectum. The rectum is about 30 centimeters in length before it exits the body by the anus.

The large intestine has numerous tissue bands that can often be felt on rectal examination. These tissue bands can serve as a guide in identifying what piece of intestine is being felt during rectal examination. The cecum and right and left ventral colon are segments that have four bands. The left dorsal colon has one band. The right dorsal colon has three bands, and the small colon has two bands. The small intestine does not have these soft tissue bands.

Other abdominal cavity contents are similar to those found in other mammals. These include the bladder and associated ureters, kidneys, spleen, liver, pancreas, major vessels, etc. Not all of these structures can be identified on rectal examination (see section on rectal examination, page 37), but many may be visualized by ultrasound examination.

## DIGESTION IN THE HORSE

The horse's evolution as a forage eater helps in understanding its digestive system, which is designed for continuous grazing of grass forages. The stomach and the small intestine can receive a nearly continuous flow of small amounts of food. The large intestine has been adapted to extract extra nutrition from the fiber content of the forages that pass through the small intestine.

Domestication of the horse is at odds with an intestinal system well developed for continual grazing. Convenience to owners, modern equine athletic activities, and space limitations dictate modern feeding practices and force horses to receive more concentrated feeds at infrequent intervals, harvested and processed forages, and reduced access to pasture that permits natural grazing. Cereal grains and fats have, therefore, been artificially increased in the diets of domesticated horses. Because the intestinal tract is not "designed" for this type of feeding, we see more digestive disturbances in horses receiving these modern management and feeding practices.

Although the anatomy of the equine intestinal tract is not dissimilar from that of other mammals, its organization and physiologic function differ. From the mouth to the beginning of the large intestine at the segment called the cecum, the digestive tract functions similarly to that of humans. However, the horse has a comparatively reduced capacity for digestion.

Salivary digestion of carbohydrates occurs in humans and other species, but such digestion is minimal in horses. Beyond the cecum, the large intestine functions more like that of the forestomachs of a ruminant such as a cow. In the cecum and large intestine there is continual fermentation of dietary fiber. Normal function of the hindgut (intestinal tract beyond the small intestine) of the horse is highly dependent on an adequate source of dietary fiber, and without it the horse is at risk of developing various dietary imbalances.

As in humans, a horse's digestion process begins in the mouth, where grasping of food and manipulation and chewing by the lips, tongue, and teeth allow grinding of feed into smaller pieces. This is particularly important for efficient digestion of fibrous feeds such as hay and for grinding and digestion of whole grains. For this reason dental care is important to the horse in order to facilitate adequate digestion of feeds and to maintain body condition. Dental problems may lead to dropping of clumps of feed material from the mouth (quidding) and may predispose horses to choke (esophageal obstruction) and impaction colic.

Rate of digestion is determined by feed type. For instance, horses may take more than a half hour to eat one kilogram of hay, while the consumption of a similar amount of concentrated feed will take as little as 10 minutes. This translates into a significant difference in the amount of time the horse on a concentrated diet versus one on forage or a pasture diet spends eating. Less time spent eating reportedly has been associated with increased boredom and development of vices.

Chewing produces saliva. Because eating hay requires more chewing time, saliva production for hay is greater than for grains or concentrate. Saliva, which is high in bicarbonate, moistens the feed and helps to buffer acid secretions in the stomach. Therefore, diets containing adequate hay and/or pasture forage produce higher levels of salivary secretion and decrease the risk of developing gastric ulcers. Saliva production is nearly two times greater for hay or grass than for grains and concentrates.

Once the food enters the stomach, digestion begins. However, only a limited amount of digestion occurs in the stomach. In reality, the stomach primarily functions to liquefy the feed in preparation for passage into the small intestine. The limited digestion that occurs is primarily for initial break-down of proteins by an enzyme called pepsin. Because the stomach produces acid continuously, continual grazing permits increased protection from gastric ulcers by the bicarbonate introduced from salivary secretions. Continual grazing also permits absorption of gastric juices by feedstuff that is always in the stomach. Horses that are fed concentrated diets and do not graze in between the concentrate "meals" probably have long periods of time when there is little or no bicarbonate being introduced from the saliva. Nor do they have feed in the stomach to absorb the gastric juices. This type of feeding can predispose horses to ulcer development.

True extraction and absorption of nutrients begin in the small intestine. Ingesta (the liquefied feed material released from the stomach into the small intestine) passes through the small intestine rather quickly. Some ingesta may reach the cecum in one hour, and most will reach this site by three hours after ingestion. Things such as meal size, type of feed, and activity level can influence the transit time through the small intestine, the primary site for digestion and absorption of sugar and starch (a complex sugar). The most important source of sugar in the horse's diet comes from pasture grasses. A significant source of dietary sugar may also come from sun-cured hay, but hay forage has an overall lower sugar content relative to pasture grass. Some sweet feeds contain up to 10% molasses; therefore, another major source of dietary sugar may also be in the form of the sugar present in molasses.

Starch is a complex form of a carbohydrate in plants that is broken down to produce sugar. A tremendous number of sugar (glucose) molecules make up the complex structure of the starch molecule in plants. Therefore, the breakdown (digestion) of starch in feed releases large amounts of sugar for absorption. Starch is a major component of cereal grains. Oats are about 50% starch and corn may be up to 70% starch in content. The simple sugars in molasses and grasses are easily digested by the horse. However, starch, because of its molecular complexity, requires breakdown into less complex sugars that can be further broken down into simple sugars before they can be absorbed like the simple sugars found in molasses and grasses. Amylase is an enzyme that is released into the duodenum from the pancreas (through the pancreatic duct) that initiates the digestion of complex sugar molecules such as starch. However, amylase is produced in limited amounts in the horse, relative to other species. Therefore, the small intestine of the horse can become overwhelmed by excess dietary starch. As a general rule, a single grain or concentrate meal should be no greater than 5 pounds in weight. Furthermore, the digestibility of starch also varies among different types of grain. For instance, starch in corn is rather poorly digestible. However, grains in most commercially produced feeds are processed to improve the digestibility of starch within them. Despite this processing, there is always significant risk that with large grain meals undigested starch may reach the large intestine. This can be associated with digestive disturbances in the large intestine. Furthermore, heavy grain meals result in rapid transit through the stomach and small intestine. Increased rapidity of transit through the small intestine reduces time for the small intestine to digest and absorb available starch. Therefore, in addition to the increased levels of starch in heavy grain meals, the transit of starch to the large intestine is further facilitated by reduced time for starch digestion. Pelleted and ground feeds move through faster than hay and grass feeds. The fat-soluble vitamins (A, D, E, K), calcium, and phosphorous are also absorbed in the small intestine and a horse's daily requirements of vitamins and minerals are usually met when it ingests a minimum of 3 pounds of a commercially produced concentrated feed. However, for many horses these requirements can be met simply by feeding high-quality hay or having access to good pasture.

Fat and protein digestion also occurs predominantly in the small intestine. Enzymes from the pancreas and in the lining of the small intestine are capable of digesting proteins to their individual amino acids, permitting their absorption into the bloodstream. The horse's diet is usually relatively low in fat, yet horses do have the capacity to digest and absorb large quantities of this nutrient. Studies of fat in the equine diet have indicated that horses can tolerate up to 10% of their total diet as dietary fat.

Once ingesta has passed through the small intestine, the material moves into the large intestine. This begins with the cecum. Attached to the cecum is the remainder of the large intestine (described in the anatomy section). Similar to the rumen of a cow, the cecum and large colon are "fermentation vats" where microorganisms including bacteria and protozoa perform much of the digestion by producing enzymes capable of breaking down fiber. This digestion, which does not occur in humans, enables any fermenting species to break down structural sugars in the fibrous portion of the diet. The process takes much more time than the digestive process described for the small intestine. Ingesta that enter the large intestine may remain there for up to 48 hours before being passed as fecal material. The dietary fiber in the feed is not capable of being digested by the horse's own digestive enzymes. Dietary fiber is primarily made up of the structural components of plant material; mammalian digestive processes cannot use this energy source. However, because of the symbiotic relationship between the microorganisms and the horse (or other fermenting species), cellulose and hemicellulose that exist in plants are broken down and available for use as energy. Lignin, another form of fiber, cannot be broken down by fermentation. Therefore, it is passed in the feces. For this reason the type of dietary fiber influences its nutritional value. Overly mature hay will have relatively high amounts of lignin, which reduces its digestibility and, therefore, its value as a dietary source of nutrients and energy. However, young hay, beet pulp, and soy hulls have much less lignin and much more digestible fiber. They are, therefore, much more valuable to the horse as an energy source.

The fermentation process leads to the production of a group of compounds called volatile fatty acids. They are produced by the digestion of the digestible dietary fiber. These volatile fatty acids are acetate, butyrate, and proprionate. In addition to these compounds, heat, water, and gas are also produced. These volatile fatty acids can be absorbed into the bloodstream, where they are an extremely important source of energy for the horse. Vitamin K is a by-product of the activity of the microorganisms in the large intestine. It becomes available to horses for absorption by their activity. Horses, therefore, seldom require vitamin K in their diet. The microorganisms in the large colon and cecum also break down protein that enters the large intestine. However, this protein is not used by the horse; rather, the end product of this breakdown is ammonia. Ammonia is then used by the bacteria to produce protein required for the bacteria's growth and survival — thus the symbiotic relationship (both the bacteria and the horse benefit). The digestive process essentially ends at this point in the large intestine. The remainder of absorption that takes place is primarily absorption of water in order to recover the fluid secreted to aid digestion and passage of ingesta. The end result is the formation of concentrated fecal balls of waste left over from the digestive processes.

Having reviewed some of the anatomically and physiologically significant factors that are important in the process of digestion and intestinal transit of feedstuff through the equine gastrointestinal system, you will be better able to understand many factors that may be controlled to help prevent colic and some of the processes that may become disrupted when a horse experiences an episode of colic.

# CHAPTER 1

## *Defining Colic*

It is important to define the word colic in order to understand its meaning, as it pertains to the horse. A common misconception is that colic is a specific diagnosis associated with a well-defined cause. However, colic is, in reality, merely a clinical sign and not a diagnosis. The term colic actually means, in the broadest sense, abdominal pain. Abdominal pain is relatively common, even in people. We tend to refer to our abdominal pain as "stomach aches." Most of the time when people get "stomach aches," we have no idea what has specifically taken place to cause the pain. We also realize that we are likely to recover from the discomfort without medical (or surgical) intervention. Therefore, we often never discover the cause of our "stomach aches." In horses, numerous conditions, both specific and non-specific, may also lead to abdominal pain, yet most of these conditions go undiagnosed because of the self-limiting nature of most of the causes of colic. Colic is the manifestation of the cause of abdominal pain and not a specific diagnosis of its cause.

Although animals and humans experience abdominal pain (colic), horses, for many reasons, seem especially prone to conditions that lead to colic. These reasons have been discussed in the introduction.

Any condition that leads to the disruption of normal intestinal motility (lack of motility or increased or disorganized motility) can result in fluid and gas accumulation in the intestine. If this condition persists, the intestines, because of their poor attachments to the abdominal wall, may move to places where they do not normally belong. On their way to these abnormal locations, the intestines may twist or simply become lodged or trapped in areas that do not allow for the normal removal of the intestinal contents and gas. In some situations such twisting or entrapments can also lead to the restriction or complete blockage of normal blood flow to and/or from a segment of the intestine. Primary inflammatory conditions of the intestine (enteritis) may also affect the intestines, leading to disrupted motility and dysfunction of the affected segment. The disruption of intestinal function can itself lead to motility changes, pain, and abnormal function of other areas not directly affected by the inflammatory process. Inflammatory conditions may also affect the intestine secondary to intestinal displacement and/or restriction of the blood supply. Therefore, a condition causing "colic" can cause a cycle of displacement, inflammation, loss of normal function and blood supply, and pain. However, it is important to realize that movement of intestine to abnormal locations, entrapments, inflammation, loss of blood supply, and twists (volvulus) are not necessary in order for colic to take place.

> ## AT A GLANCE
>
> - Colic means abdominal pain. It is not a specific diagnosis.
>
> - The intestine can twist or become trapped in areas it does not belong.
>
> - A number of risk factors are associated with increased incidence of colic, including a history of colic, changes in feeding programs, poor parasite control, and poor dental care.

## THE INCIDENCE OF COLIC

The good news is that most horses that experience colic do not usually reach the point where this cycle cannot be broken. Indeed, the vast majority of colic episodes resolve with no or minimal veterinary intervention. The incidence of equine colic has been estimated by the USDA's National Animal Health Monitoring System Equine 1998 study at 4.2 events per 100 horses per year. This health monitoring system was designed to outline the overall prevalence and occurrence of various types of disease within the North American horse population. The 1998 study found no difference in the incidence of colic among geographic regions. The percentage of equine operations that experienced one or more colic events was 16.3. Overall, only 1.4% of colic events resulted in surgical intervention. The fatality rate for all colic events was 11%.

In this same report neither gender nor use of horse was associated with the incidence of colic. There does, however, appear to be some association between some *types* of colic and gender. For instance, uterine torsion and scrotal herniation would be expected to be gender specific. Furthermore, colonic torsion (twisting of the large intestine) appears to be more prevalent in mares. Nonetheless, gender is not consistently a factor that affects incidence of other causes of colic.

Although gender is not a major factor in colic, the study did suggest some breeds may appear more susceptible. The NAHMS study found Thoroughbreds are more likely to develop colic (10.9 colic events per 100 horses per year) than stock horse breeds such as Quarter Horses, Paints, and Appaloosas (3.5 colic events per 100 horses per year) or other types of horses (2.9 colic events per 100 horses per year). According to several other epidemiological studies, Arabians and younger miniature horses appear to exhibit a higher incidence of colic due to fecaliths (accretions or "stones" of fecal material formed within the intestines) and small colon impactions, while Standardbreds might have a higher incidence of scrotal hernias. The studies did not cite specific reasons for these associations. However, it is important to realize that factors other than breed might account for the heightened incidence in certain breeds. Owners of certain types of horses may be more observant of signs of colic, and various breeds may be managed and monitored differently. A genetic predisposition to certain gastrointestinal disorders could also be possible.

Age, too, may affect the incidence of colic. Age group evaluation in the NAHMS study found the following facts:

• Foals less than six months exhibited colic at a rate of 0.2 events per 100 horses per year.

• Horses between six and 18 months exhibited 4.5 events per 100 horses per year.

• Horses 18 months to five years exhibited 5.9 events per 100 horses per year.

• Horses five years to 20 years exhibited 4.2 colic events per 100 horses per year.

• Horses older than 20 experienced 4.2 colic events per 100 horses per year.

## RISK FACTORS FOR COLIC

A number of risk factors are associated with increased incidence of colic. Horses that have a history of colic occurrences and/or previous colic surgery might be more likely to exhibit future bouts. Management factors might also affect the likelihood of colic episodes. Dietary management practices such as using certain types of feed, increased amounts of feed, and increased concentrations of feed may be associated with higher incidences of colic, laminitis (a painful foot condition), and endotoxemia, a condition in which toxins are released from dying bacteria (cell walls) within the body and circulated in the blood. Changes in the diet, such as in the type and/or quality of feed and hay or other dietary forage, might lead to higher colic incidence.

In reality, a limited number of risk factors for colic can be directly controlled by owner intervention. Using good feeding practices and dietary management, parasite control, and good health practices are probably the extent of our ability to minimize the risk factors for colic in the horse. Although specific and predictable relationships of feeding practices to the incidence of colic are often unclear, dietary management is universally considered to be important when evaluating risk factors associated with developing colic. Furthermore, constant access to fresh, palatable water is also universally regarded as a controllable facet of management that may significantly impact the incidence of colic.

The incidence of colic may be associated with the manner in which horses are housed. Horses in densely populated environments, horses that are being moved from pasture to a stall, and horses with unrestricted access to *lush* pasture may all be at increased risk of colic. Horses that are kept on pasture or that spend more time grazing, provided the grass is not too lush, seem to exhibit fewer colic episodes.

Changes in activity levels have been associated with colic. However, the specific relationship of activity to colic incidence is poorly defined and speculative. There may be an association of increased incidence of colic with exercise at either extreme (lack of exercise and highly intense exercise).

Regular dental care is thought to be an important component in preventing colic. However, there is no concrete documentation of this association. Poor mastication can lead to maldigestion, esophageal obstructions, and intestinal impactions. For these reasons (and others) it is advisable your horse(s) receive regular dental care.

Regular deworming is also considered to be important in the prevention of colic. Generally speaking, colic episodes are likely to be fewer on farms that practice good parasite control. However, the manner in which a successful parasite control program is instituted varies greatly and depends on farm management practices, horse density, geographic location, and economics. Often, parasite control programs are designed to minimize the cyathostome (small strongyle) infections in horses. The larval forms of cyathostome parasites can encyst in the equine intestine and are often associated with increased colic episodes and/or overall poor health. Tapeworm infestations may occur less frequently but have also been associated with various types of colic such as intus-susception, ileal impaction, and spasmodic colic (see Chapter 3). While parasites can trigger colic, deworming medications also have been implicated in inducing colic, but whether a specific medication is more likely to cause colic is unclear. Although there is no real evidence of this relationship, a recent deworming could be associated with colic episodes.

The debate continues and conclusions vary about the effect of ambient temperatures and weather on the incidence of colic. Warmer conditions have been associated with increased dehydration and, subsequently, increased incidence of colic. Colder temperatures have been associated with a reduced amount of water consumption and increased incidence of colic. Overall, clear association between such environmental factors as temperatures, temperature changes, rainfall, or barometric pressure and the incidence of colic has not been shown on a repeatable basis. Nonetheless, clinical experience and some epidemiologic evidence suggest an association between temperature variables and colic incidence.

Some specific horse behaviors have been suggested to cause colic. Cribbing is commonly believed to lead to colic through the "swallowing" of air that might accumulate in the stomach and intestines. Despite this common belief, no clear evidence links cribbing to colic. Nonetheless, it is worthwhile to minimize cribbing regardless of any association with colic, since it is destructive to the horse's teeth and to the objects on which the horse cribs. Wood chewing and pica (indiscriminate consumption of non-food items) may lead to colic from digestive upset and foreign body obstruction. Pica is probably more common in younger horses, and horses that chew wood may be lacking dietary roughage.

The cause(s) of any colic episode often goes undiagnosed. Many times colic episodes may be initiated by a combination of factors. Although some factors are believed to play an associative role in increasing colic incidence, the reality is most colic episodes occur due to undefined causes and all or none of the above risk factors for colic may be at work for any one episode.

## WHAT'S HAPPENING TO THE INTESTINE DURING A COLIC EPISODE?

In a very general sense the intestine responds to "upset" in predictable ways. The manifestation of the clinical signs of colic probably depends on the initial inciting event(s) and the degree to which normal intestinal physiology and function are disrupted. Intestinal inflammation often becomes involved in this disruption, further adding to a self-perpetuating cycle of intestinal dysfunction. Inflammation may be primary (as in an inflammatory intestinal condition) or secondary (e.g., as a result of loss of blood supply, strangulation, and/or displacement). As we have alluded already, the inciting event(s) of colic may be poorly defined in most colic cases. Furthermore, they are likely to be multi-faceted. Regardless of the initial inciting cause of a colic episode, the disruption of intestinal physiology and function leads to alterations in intestinal motility, gas distension of the intestine, changes in blood supply and blood drainage, edema (tissue fluid accumulation), and physical destruction of the inside surface of the intestine, which normally helps to mediate absorption of water and nutritional elements.

Along with and because of intestinal dysfunction, horses can exhibit pain for several other reasons. Abdominal pain can often be termed "visceral pain" or pain associated with the abdominal organs. This pain may be of various intensities and difficult to pinpoint. Parietal pain is another type of pain associated with a colic episode and with diseases that affect the abdominal cavity itself rather than the organs within it. Depending on the cause of the colic and its severity, both types of pain may occur. These types of pain are difficult or impossible to distinguish by clinical signs alone. Visceral pain receptors are abundant in the intestines themselves and are sensitive to stretching, traction (pulling), and strong muscular contractions or other tension. Inflammation may also lead to visceral pain by direct, pain-causing substances that accumulate with intestinal inflammation or by loss of blood supply (ischemia). Therefore, poor or disorganized motility can cause pain because of the loss of normal intestinal function, gas and fluid accumulation, and/or accumulation of intestinal contents that fail to move through the intestinal tract. Primary intestinal inflammation and primary intestinal obstructions can also induce pain and intestinal motility changes. Pain and other related intestinal nervous system responses have also been shown to have negative effects on intestinal motility. These changes further amplify overall intestinal dysfunction that can lead to inflammation and further worsen intestinal motility.

Despite the potential for a self-enhancing cascade of events, not all colic episodes are destined to reach a point of self-perpetuating physiological dysfunction. Indeed, for many colic episodes, the inciting cause may not reach the level of severity or may not persist for a long enough period to initiate the cycle. If some of the events of this cycle do take place, they still have the potential to resolve on their own or with relatively simple intervention before they lead to the stage at which the inflammation perpetuates the intestinal dysfunction, which itself may add to the inflammatory process. Simultaneous existence of factors (such as edema, motility disturbance, altered blood supply, accumulated ingesta, etc.) in this cycle probably increases the likelihood that the condition worsens and requires more intensive intervention. The presence of some of the more serious factors on their own, such as the loss of blood supply, may necessitate intensive intervention.

In more serious colic episodes or intestinal disturbances, the inner intestinal lining (mucosa) may become damaged by inflammation and/or inadequate blood supply (ischemia). Once this happens, endotoxemia can result from the loss of the integrity of the lining that normally acts as a barrier to bacteria and their toxins (endotoxins). Although it can be caused by conditions other than intestinal disease, endotoxemia (the presence of endotoxin from bacteria in the blood) is relatively common in cases of intestinal disturbances that lead to bacterial release of endotoxin and to the subsequent absorption of this toxin into the blood through the damaged intestinal lining (mucosa).

The bacterial organisms can cause a dramatic biochemical response that leads to a significant release of inflammatory mediators throughout the entire body (shock). Their release may lead to poor blood perfusion of the tissues throughout the body, abnormal blood clotting, and even death. Endotoxemia has been implicated in the development of laminitis in horses. Horses with severe diarrhea and other serious intestinal disturbances, such as strangulating obstructions and severe inflammation of the large and small intestine, commonly encounter endotoxemia.

## THE CLINICAL SIGNS OF COLIC IN THE HORSE

Clinical signs of colic are those changes in behavior or activity that indicate abdominal pain. Although these signs are relatively universal, individual horses may exhibit slightly different cues and different intensities to the same causes of colic. For instance, a colicky foal often rolls onto its back with its feet in the air. Some older horses and perhaps certain breeds may be more stoic than others. Such horses may experience abdominal pain and show few

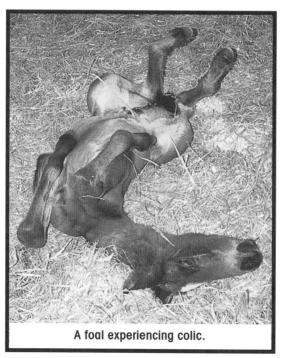

**A foal experiencing colic.**

obvious signs of this pain other than depression or unwillingness to move. Overall, no one knows when a horse is behaving abnormally better than an owner who is well acquainted with his/her horse's normal behavior. Such individuals may pick up on early or subtle behavioral changes that could indicate a problem. Changes that owners often recognize early may include increased recumbency, failure to finish grain or hay, reduced activity either in the stall or in the pasture, increased time spent lying down, abnormal stance, increased time required for feed consumption, reduced fecal production, dry or loose feces, poor hair coat, and weight loss.

These changes are important to share with your veterinarian, who does not have the benefit of seeing these day-to-day changes in your horse. Therefore, the owner serves as the eyes and ears to the episodes that have prompted veterinary intervention. Your veterinarian can use this information to help evaluate your horse. As important as this information is, you, as the owner, need to realize that these subtle changes in your horse are not specific to any one condition. Therefore, these signs do not necessarily mean that your horse is experiencing colic.

Your veterinarian will perform a complete examination

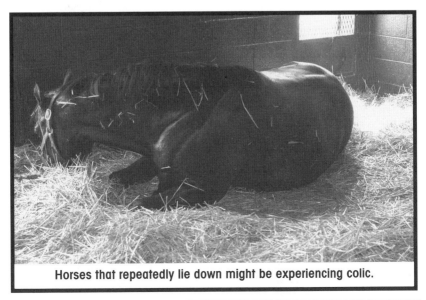

**Horses that repeatedly lie down might be experiencing colic.**

that may seem to include things that do not focus on the intestinal system. This is the correct approach since these signs can indicate problem(s) in areas other than the intestinal tract. During the examination your veterinarian will also look for evidence of previous colic episodes such as skin abrasions, swollen and reddened skin around the eyes and over the hips (from trauma due to rolling), presence or absence of feces in the stall, scrapes left in the stall floor bedding (from pawing), and scrapes or hair found on the walls of the stall that may be left from a horse that has been cast or otherwise trying to alleviate discomfort.

Most horses will manifest abdominal pain clinically with some important signs. Very mild abdominal pain might only be apparent in the behavioral changes suggested above. However, horses with mild abdominal pain often show one or more of the following clinical signs:

- pawing at the ground with a forelimb
- stretching out
- reaching around with the head to the flank
- increased amount of time lying down
- poor appetite
- playing in the water bucket
- continual shifting of weight on the hind limbs
- standing against a wall and moving infrequently

If abdominal pain continues or if the condition causes more than simply mild abdominal pain, the signs of more intense (moderate) abdominal pain may become evident. The signs include the following actions:

- persistent movement (even in the stall)
- frequently pawing at the ground with a forelimb
- repetitively lying down and then getting back up
- rolling after lying down
- grunting
- kicking at the belly
- frequently turning the head to the flank

Clinical manifestations of severe abdominal pain may

include the following signs or behaviors:

- profuse sweating
- continuous rolling
- persistent movement
- getting up and down violently

These lists are only general guidelines for gauging the severity of pain. Indeed, individual horses might display other manifestations of pain. Furthermore, the signs of colic displayed by any horse do not neatly divide into the three levels of pain presented here. For any colicky horse several signs from any of the above lists may be present, or there may be few or none if the horse is particularly stoic.

With more advanced progression of colic or with certain types of colic, horses might become more depressed than painful. Depression is generally believed to occur as blood flow decreases to the intestine and leads to segmental death of intestinal tissue and endotoxemia, dehydration, and other poor blood perfusion of the body tissues that can be associated with poor oxygen delivery to the same tissues. Many types of inflammatory diseases of the intestine produce more depression than pain. Anterior enteritis, colitis, and peritonitis may be more likely to cause greater depression than abdominal pain without necessarily being associated with death of the intestine.

Other than in the instances noted above, greater abdominal pain (colic) is generally associated with more severe disease. Therefore, strangulation of a segment of intestine that leads to loss of blood supply and intestinal death causes more pain than an impaction that causes intestinal obstruction. However, gas distension of any segment of intestine can be extremely painful due to continuous stretching and tension on the intestine and its attachment to the body wall (the mesentery). If severe abdominal pain that has been evident gives way to acute relief and comfort, the astute veterinarian is usually considering the possibility of a rupture of a distended segment of intestine (stomach or intestinal rupture).

## CHAPTER 2

# *The Colic Examination*

The purpose of this section is to familiarize the reader with the whys and hows of the colic examination. This section will not make the horse owner an expert on the colic exam. Indeed, this section is likely to provide information on many more approaches and techniques used for colic examinations than are required for any one exam. In many situations the equine veterinarian must be experienced enough with colic to "streamline" the examination in the interest of time and to make good, expedient decisions. For this reason it is uncommon to see all of the described techniques and procedures being performed in every colic situation. This does not mean the owner's horse is getting an inadequate examination. Many of the procedures described are not appropriate for every type of colic episode. The veterinarian must evaluate the case, identify (if possible) the type of colic present, and then decide on the need for each of the available diagnostic techniques and procedures. These diagnostics and procedures and their indications will be described further.

One of the most important questions for a veterinarian to answer is whether he/she believes the horse will require referral to an institution at which intensive medical or surgical intervention is available. For some colic episodes the answer to this question may be more obvious than for others.

However, the answer is neither always obvious nor easy. Numerous factors must be considered before deciding upon referral. These factors are covered later in this book.

## IMPORTANT OBSERVATIONS

A history of the events that preceded the colic examination often provides valuable information in interpreting the findings. A detailed history may not be practical or possible in an emergency. However, any history of previous health problems (including colic), the age, lems (including colic), the age, breed, and sex of the horse, the duration of the clinical signs, the severity and frequency of the colic episodes, fecal production, and the time the horse was last judged to be normal are helpful information the owner should try to provide. Nutrition may also be an appropriate topic to address, since it is believed that changes in feeding or other factors of nutrition may be involved in the development of colic. Access to sand and/or poor-quality forage is noteworthy. In certain geographic areas, feeding improperly cured alfalfa hay may be linked to colic associated with blister beetles. An owner should provide the history and specific practices of deworming. Access to clean, palatable water is important and should be addressed by either indirect examination or specific discussion with the veterinarian. Owners/caretakers of mares that experience colic should provide breeding histories and stages of pregnancy to the examining veterinarian.

It is imperative to tell the veterinarian about any and all medications administered to the horse, as interpretation of the examination findings is likely to be affected by these medications. A horse that appears to be comfortable during the examination but has received repetitive doses of medication is clearly different than a horse that has received no

### AT A GLANCE

- A general physical examination is an important part of a clinical evaluation for colic.

- Ultrasound is the most common diagnostic imaging technique used in colic examinations.

- Nasogastric intubation should never be performed by a lay person.

medication. However, these two horses may be clinically indistinguishable unless the medication history is provided.

## THE PHYSICAL EXAMINATION

A general physical examination is performed as part of the clinical evaluation of the horse exhibiting colic. This examination is termed "general" because it focuses on examination parameters that are not specific for conditions most often associated with a colic episode. However, these parameters are important in evaluating the overall current health status of the horse (i.e., how stable the animal is at the time of the examination). The parameters most likely to be evaluated include a rectal temperature, heart rate, respiratory rate, capillary refill time, and an evaluation of the mucous membrane color. The rectal temperature must be taken before performing any rectal examination because air introduced into the rectum will falsely lower the temperature. The normal rectal temperature should usually be below 101 degrees Fahrenheit. Normal rectal temperatures of foals tend to be slightly higher but

The veterinarian listens to the abdomen.

should generally be below 102 degrees Fahrenheit. Increases in body temperature may occur in a normal animal after activity, excitement, or anxiety. However, body temperatures greater than 103 degrees often suggest an inflammatory and/or infectious condition that may be directly associated with or be the cause of colic. Colic conditions commonly associated with fevers include anterior enteritis, peritonitis, colitis, and intestinal rupture. Low body temperatures are often seen with severe circulatory disturbance and shock.

The heart rate, respiratory rate, mucous membrane color and moisture, and capillary refill time help the veterinarian determine such things as the degree of pain (by heart rate and respiratory rate) and compromise of general body blood flow and distribution (by heart rate, mucous membrane color, and capillary refill time). A horse with severe disturbance of blood flow due to dehydration, loss of fluid into the intestinal tract, uneven and poorly coordinated blood distribution, and endotoxemia would be expected to exhibit a high heart rate and dark red to purple dry mucous membranes with a slow capillary refill time (three seconds or more). Such a horse may also exhibit a high respiratory rate due to body acid/base disturbance and/or pain. Other parameters of hydration may be evaluated, but their interpretation can be highly subjective if the state of dehydration is not severe. Findings that may further indicate dehydration include prolonged skin tenting after being pinched on the shoulder or neck, slow jugular vein filling after holding it off at the base of the neck, sunken eyes, depression, and high heart rate. A high heart rate is also indicative of abdominal pain but can also be due to several other factors, including dehydration and endotoxemia. The relative significance of all factors that may affect the heart rate must be interpreted in light of the other clinical findings.

After, or along with, the initial evaluation, the veterinarian usually listens to the abdomen (auscults) for evidence of rumbling sounds that indicate intestinal movement (termed borborygmi). This evaluation is subjective. The examining veterinarian notes whether there is lack of intestinal sounds. If sounds are present, then the veterinarian notes the frequency of intestinal sounds as an indication of intestinal motility, their intensity, and location. Although this examination may help ascertain an overall impression of intestinal motility, it is not very specific. On occasion, an experienced veterinarian might hear the sound of sand moving in the intestines. These "sand sounds" are subjectively assessed and more likely to be heard in horses that live in areas with large amounts of sand in the soil. Otherwise, much of the information from abdominal auscultation serves only to answer very general questions regarding intestinal motility. These questions may include the following: 1) Is there any motility? 2) Does the motility sound organized? 3) Is the motility uniform throughout the abdomen? 4) Is the motility decreasing or increasing in intensity, duration, and frequency? 5) Are there any sounds that may indicate a large gas viscus (an intestinal accumulation of gas)? This last question is often addressed by simple auscultation and by abdominal percussion using a finger-flicking motion to the abdominal wall. A gas-distended viscus produces a "ping" sound, similar to the sound of a playground ball that "pings" as it hits the pavement.

## NASOGASTRIC INTUBATION

Another component of the colic examination can be considered diagnostic as well as therapeutic. This procedure is nasogastric intubation, or "tubing" as it is commonly termed. This procedure involves inserting a stomach tube into the nose and running the tube down the back of the throat and esophagus and into the stomach. This procedure can be technically difficult to perform and should not be performed by any lay person. Improper tubing can result in water, oil, or other substances getting into the lungs; loss of the tube into the stomach; esophageal rupture; and other complications.

One complication relatively common in horses that are difficult to tube is a nosebleed. Horses that throw their heads or are difficult to tube are at greater risk of nosebleeds, but the procedure can cause bleeding in any horse. Owners often become highly distressed when their horses have nose bleeds. Bleeding often appears to be very severe, and it is not uncommon for an owner to ask if the horse will need a blood transfusion. Although the volume of blood lost appears to be great in a number of these cases, the red blood cell indices of these horses do not change significantly. It may be helpful to remember that the horse is a large animal and has a much larger blood volume than people do, often in excess of 40 liters compared to about 5 liters in people. Horses with nose-

bleeds may bleed for some time due to the highly vascular nature of the nasal lining, but nosebleeds almost always stop with simple rest and, in future nasogastric intubation, avoidance of the nostril that bled.

The nasogastric tube is usually passed to check for reflux (accumulation of fluid and/or feedstuff on the stomach). This procedure helps to tell the veterinarian if the stomach is emptying and/or if the

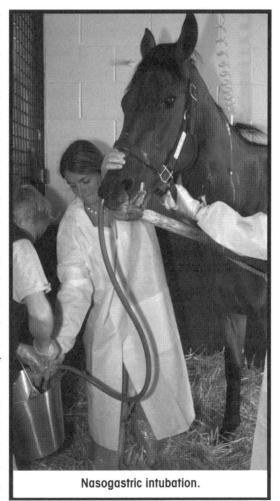

**Nasogastric intubation.**

small intestine is moving fluid and ingesta away from the stomach. If these functions are not happening normally, there may be substantial amounts of fluid on the stomach. Nasogastric intubation is particularly important in horses because they do not have the ability to regurgitate. Fluid and ingesta may accumulate in the stomach because the horse is incapable of vomiting. This fluid must therefore manually be removed with a nasogastric tube to prevent spontaneous re-fluxing of the accumulated fluid up the esophagus and out of the nose due to the pressure from the overdistended stomach. If nasogastric intubation is not performed, pressure continues to develop in the stomach and the horse is at risk of stomach rupture. Horses with severe fluid accumulation may reflux spontaneously from the nose due to backpressure created by excess fluid and gas. Spontaneous reflux from the nose is not normal and, unfortunately, does not provide enough pressure release from the stomach to prevent stomach rupture. Spontaneous reflux from the stomach, therefore, indicates severe pressure in the stomach. The reflux that reaches the top of the esophagus can be aspirated into the trachea and lungs. Thus, spontaneous reflux must be immediately treated by nasogastric intubation of the stomach to prevent both aspi-ration pneumonia in the lungs and possible stomach rupture. Fluid accumulation can cause significant pain and stretching of the stomach and, ultimately, rupture of the stomach. Obstructions that can cause fluid stasis in the stomach include any strangulating physical obstructions of the intes-tine downstream from the stomach, most commonly small in-testinal physical obstructions (small intestinal volvulus, stran-gulating lipoma, etc.), or functional obstructions in which the loss of normal intestinal function and motility leads to fluid and ingesta accumulation.

Nasogastric intubation is also performed to administer several therapeutic compounds. These include water, elec-trolytes and water, mineral oil, dioctyl sodiumsulfosuccinate (DSS), magnesium sulfate (epsom salts), psyllium hydrophilic mucilloid (Metamucil®), and others. These compounds will be addressed in the section that covers therapeutic management of colic. It is imperative to realize that it can be extremely dangerous to attempt to tube your own horse or to have an untrained individual perform this procedure. Due to inappropriate placement of nasogastric tubes through the esophagus and into the chest cavity, horses have died from mineral oil deposited into the lungs and from other major complications. Furthermore, severe nasal, pharyngeal, and esophageal trauma can occur, and nasogastric tubes can slip out of the hand of the person operating the tube and be subsequently lost into the lungs or into the stomach.

## THE RECTAL EXAMINATION

A rectal examination is another component of the colic examination. When a rectal examination is performed, the veterinarian is able to feel only about one-third or slightly more of the abdominal contents through the rectal wall. In other words, all of the abdomen is palpated with the tissue of the rectum overlying the hand of the examiner. The information provided by this examination is not always specific. Indeed, even a veterinarian experienced in rectal palpation may not be able to garner more information other than large or small intestinal distension, large intestinal displacement, impaction of the large intestine (intestinal overfill of the large intestine), twisting of large intestinal bands or, occasionally, evidence of intestinal herniation (such as into the scrotum of a stallion). Some palpable specific structures that the veterinarian will seek to identify may include the pelvic flexure of the large intestine, the cecum and ventral band of the cecum, the tail of the spleen, the left kidney, the ligament between the kidney and the spleen, and the bladder. Finding twisted bands of the large intestine often helps to localize and to identify the cause of a colic episode. There may only be an overall impression of normal versus abnormal rectal findings relative to the veterinarian's experience.

Although some veterinarians advocate rectal examination of every horse that exhibits colic, such an approach may be unwarranted and even dangerous to some horses. Horses that do not exhibit abdominal pain and have a normal physical examination might be appropriately dismissed from the rectal examination. Furthermore, young and/or fractious horses that appear to be otherwise normal by examination pose significant potential danger for rectal tears. Consequently, the veterinarian must weigh the relative benefits of the rectal examination versus the danger for rectal tears. Horses that do not receive rectal examination should not have gastric reflux when the nasogastric tube is passed.

Performing a rectal examination requires some precautions to minimize the dangers of rectal tears. Such precautions include appropriate restraint and twitching of the horse, performance of the examination in as confined an area as is physically possible (such as in a stall), sedation, good lubrication of the hand and arm of the examiner, and good technique that minimizes forceful introduction of the hand and arm against straining by the animal. Other techniques include the addition of lidocaine to the lubrication jelly, epidural anesthesia, and administration of small doses of propantheline to minimize intestinal smooth muscle contraction.

A veterinarian must interpret the information provided by rectal examination because the palpation findings will be useless and uninterpretable to anyone who has not received specific veterinary training. The rectal examination is always potentially dangerous but can be performed safely when proper precautions are taken and when performed by an experienced veterinarian. As an owner, you should realize that even with all of these precautions, rectal tears do happen. Horses that are being examined rectally are likely to be dehydrated, have distended and weakened intestinal walls, and be unable to stand quietly due to abdominal pain. Nonetheless, the rectal examination is generally regarded as an appropriate and necessary part of the evaluation of horses with colic.

Horses that have not received a rectal examination on the first colic exam but require a repeat examination due to persistent or recurrent colic should receive a rectal examination on the follow-up examination.

## ADDITIONAL DIAGNOSTICS

Several other procedures and diagnostics may be performed on the horse that exhibits abdominal pain. These include abdominocentesis ("belly tap"), complete blood count and serum biochemistry, ultrasonography, sand sedimentation examination, microbiology, endoscopy, laparoscopy, and exploratory celiotomy. Many of these procedures are not easily performed on a farm or barn visit due to lack of necessary equipment and personnel as well as financial considerations. Abdominocentesis and complete blood count and serum biochemistry samples can be obtained in the field. However, appropriate evaluation of these samples must take place at a veterinary hospital or laboratory that has the appropriate equipment.

### Abdominocentesis (Aspiration of Abdominal Fluid)

Abdominocentesis is performed on horses to evaluate the cell types and protein concentration of the abdominal fluid. The abdominal fluid is "sampled" by placement of a 1 1/2-inch needle into the abdomen, usually at its lowest point. Fluid is "caught" in blood tubes for evaluation of cell counts and types, cell morphology, and for protein evaluation. Longer needles may be required to obtain fluid in some instances. This procedure can provide indirect but important information regarding the presence or absence of inflammation and/or infection or bacterial contamination of the abdominal cavity. This procedure is relatively standard practice at most referral institutions and can provide further evidence of the need for surgical intervention or can indicate another non-surgical abdominal disease that requires specific medical therapy and management. The sample that is obtained might also be submitted for culture and sensitivity if there is evidence of infection within the abdominal cavity.

### Blood evaluation

At most referral centers a complete blood count and serum biochemistry are performed in the standard protocol for evaluating a horse with colic. This evaluation helps assess major organ function, may provide evidence of an infectious condition that could be associated with the colic episode, helps the inflammatory response, evidence of significant endotoxemia, and may provide evidence of dehydration and its severity. Certain clues in the blood also might indicate intestinal leakage of protein that could be directly or indirectly associated with the cause of the colic episode. Major organ function can be significantly disturbed in numerous intestinal and non-intestinal disorders. The evaluation of parameters relative to kidney, liver, and other organs can help identify organ damage that is either the primary cause of the colic or is present as secondary dysfunction to the primary cause of the colic (such as that seen with endotoxemia). Low white blood cell counts are relatively common in horses with endotoxemia and/or diarrhea. The blood count and biochemistry help indicate the overall stability of the horse. The common abnormalities on serum biochemistry include electrolyte disturbances and acid/base disturbances (usually acidosis — excess acid in the blood).

### Sand sedimentation

Sand sedimentation is easily performed by collecting fecal material and suspending it in water within a rectal sleeve (the above-the-elbow gloves veterinarians use to perform rectal examinations). Horses that have accumulated significant amounts of sand in the large intestine may pass some of it in the feces. This sand may settle into the fingers of the rectal sleeve. Finding sand that settles out with the sedimentation test often indicates sand as a potential source of colic (i.e., a sand colic).

### Microbiological sampling (Cultures)

Microbiological samples can be cultured to reveal bacterial organisms that might be associated with infectious causes of colic. Samples include abdominal fluid from abdominocentesis and fecal material in cases of diarrhea that could be associated with specific bacteria such as *Salmonella*, *Clostridia*, and other potential pathogenic bacteria. Intestinal biopsies and cultures of abdominal abscesses can also be sampled for culture and sensitivity.

### Endoscopic examination

Endoscopic examination of the esophagus and the rectum can be performed to evaluate for the presence of obstructions, strictures, diverticulae (abnormal outpouchings of the gastrointestinal tract), tears or other perforations, and inflammation and/or ulcers in association with a colic episode, persistent or recurrent colic episodes, poor appetite, slow feed consumption, dysphagia (inability to swallow and/or eat normally), straining, and retching. Endoscopic examination is also often used to monitor progress of healing of stomach ulcers. The endoscopic examination is not common in the evaluation of most classic cases of equine colic. The most common reason to perform an endoscopic examination of a horse with colic is to evaluate for the presence of gastric and, occasionally, duodenal ulcers as a cause of colic. Stomach ulcers are relatively common and probably affect the majority of performance horses to some degree. Ulcers may also occur in the large intestine. However, it is not possible to perform an endoscopic examination of a horse's large intestine because of the intestine's distance from the rectum. Although duodenal ulcers occur in horses, the duodenum is usually too far to reach with an endoscope, except in foals and small horses.

## DIAGNOSTIC IMAGING

Diagnostic imaging modalities are used to help evaluate horses with colic. These modalities may include ultrasonography, radiology, nuclear scintigraphy and computed tomography, or magnetic resonance imaging.

### Ultrasound

Ultrasound is by far the most common diagnostic imaging technique used in the colic examination. This non-invasive modality can be performed nearly anywhere because of the large number of portable machines now available. Use of ultrasound in evaluation of the horse's abdomen takes considerable veterinary experience. Even with a veterinarian's experience, the ultrasound machine has a number of inherent limitations. Depending on the ultrasound probe(s) used, the displayed image represents an incomplete picture of the abdomen. Furthermore, because a gas interface (an organ or space that is filled with gas) provides a barrier to ultrasound wave penetration, horses with significant gas distension of the intestine often cannot be evaluated beyond the surface of a gas-filled segment of intestine.

Horses with significant fluid-filled intestines can be identified easily with ultrasound provided the fluid-filled loops

**Use of ultrasound in diagnosing colic requires expertise.**

occur in areas the probe can penetrate. Intestinal motility and distension can be evaluated for both the large and small intestine. The thickness of the intestinal wall can be evaluated and measured. Such evaluation may provide added information about the presence of inflammation and edema in the intestinal wall. Certain types of colic may be diagnosed, or at least presumptively identified, using ultrasound evaluation. They include nephrosplenic entrapment (see Chapter 3, intestinal displacement), intussusception (see Chapter 3 strangulating or nonstrangulating lesions), right dorsal colitis, some abdominal abscesses, some abdominal soft tissue masses, and others. The use of the ultrasound machine often provides information on distension, filling, and appearance of specific areas such as the stomach, duodenum, cecum, small colon, and rectum. It also can provide similar information for non-specific areas of the small intestine and large intestine.

### Radiography

Radiography, when used for abdominal problems in the horse, is probably most likely to involve imaging of the esophagus, possibly with the aid of a contrast agent such as barium. Contrast agents allow the clinician to evaluate for the presence of foreign bodies or masses in the intestines and for abnormal distensions (such as diverticulae) and strictures. Contrast radiography is probably most useful for the evaluation of esophageal and rectal problems. The use of contrast radiography is expanded for foals because the entire abdomen can easily be radiographed due to the foal's size. Contrast radiography can be performed with a fluoroscope (an X-ray machine that is capable of real-time imaging) to visualize contrast material movement in real time. However, the use of a fluoroscope is size-restricted and, therefore, probably most practical for foals. Radiography of the adult horse's abdomen seldom yields useful results since the size of the adult abdomen precludes diagnostic films from being obtained, and the doses of radiation required are extremely high. However, radiographs of the adult abdomen have been used to help identify problems that stand out even on poorly exposed films. These conditions include the identification of sand in the large intestine and the presence of an enterolith (a stone that has formed within the large intestine). Contrast radiography on rare occasions might involve the vasculature rather than the intestines if there appears to be an indication of something such as an obstructed vessel.

### Nuclear Scintigraphy, CT, and MRI

The principle of nuclear scintigraphy is the uptake of a radioactive substance in metabolically active areas of bone or soft tissue where there might be inflammation and remodeling. The radioactive isotope is injected into the horse intravenously, and a gamma camera is used to "scan" the horse for radioactive emissions from such sites. Areas of inflammation and infection also can be specifically and sensitively identified by using nuclear scintigraphy. Radioisotope may also be used to label white blood cells. White cells are taken out of blood taken from the horse and the radioactive isotope is "added" to label them. The white cells are then administered to the horse, localize, and are detectable in areas of inflammation and infection. This technique is believed to be very sensitive for identifying abdominal abscesses and for detecting acute inflammatory conditions and eosinophilic enteritis (see Chapter 3, gastrointestinal infiltrative diseases). Nuclear scintigraphy is used infrequently to identify dental disease. Nuclear scintigraphy of the liver has also been performed to identify that organ's size, shape, and location. This technique requires the radioactive labeling and administration of colloid (a blood protein). Scintigraphy is obviously not a diagnostic modality that is practical for acute and/or emergency situations.

Computed tomography and magnetic resonance imaging are other diagnostic imaging modalities used for some chronic conditions. These techniques would be expected to provide detailed images of the abdomen but at this time are severely size-restricted to foals, miniature horses, and small ponies. Images produced would include a very detailed cross-sectional display of the abdomen and its contents. Because the use of these modalities is highly restricted, is costly, and requires general anesthesia, most referral centers do not have this equipment.

## GLUCOSE, LACTOSE, AND XYLOSE ABSORPTION TESTING (CARBOHYDRATE ABSORPTION TESTS)

Absorption tests help indicate whether the intestinal tract can perform one of its most important physiological functions — absorb carbohydrates from the small intestine. This diagnostic test is performed infrequently but can provide information that helps identify why a horse may be losing weight despite having adequate or excessive appetite. Most often, abnormal glucose, lactose, or xylose absorption tests are associated with some infiltrative intestinal condition that may compromise the intestine or make it incapable of absorption. Each carbohydrate listed above is used for different reasons, but all three tests, if abnormal, suggest impaired carbohydrate absorption. The sugar chosen for the test is given at the appropriate dose by nasogastric tube after an overnight fast and a pre-dose blood sample is drawn. Then blood samples are drawn at regularly timed intervals after the administration of the sugar by nasogastric tube. This is generally performed over a period of four or more hours. A graph can then be plotted that shows the increase in the blood concentration of the sugar due to absorption relative to sampling time (time from the dosing of the sugar). A flattened graph relative to normal sugar absorption indicates a possible problem in the ability to absorb the sugar from the intestine.

## SURGICAL DIAGNOSTICS

Exploratory celiotomy and laparoscopy are both surgical procedures. Although surgery is often necessary to correct some severe problems that cause colic, it is a diagnostic procedure as well, thus the term "exploratory celiotomy," or exploratory abdominal surgery. Surgical approaches are used as diagnostic procedures mainly because, despite all of the available diagnostics, we often do not know specifically what is happening inside the horse that is causing the colic episode(s). Thus, exploratory surgery is often used to get a first-hand look in the abdomen and to permit systematic evaluation of the intestines and other abdominal organs.

Laparoscopy is a technique that permits some visualization of the abdominal contents without being as invasive as the standard midline incision. In a manner of speaking, laparoscopy for the abdomen is similar to what arthroscopy is for joints. It allows for small incisions in order to introduce a laparoscope into the abdomen through which a picture is projected onto a monitor. The abdomen can be evaluated by the use of this scope, but a laparoscope has substantial limitations. The operator cannot see nearly as much of the abdomen with a laparoscope as with a standard midline incisional approach. Furthermore, the ability to manipulate or oth-

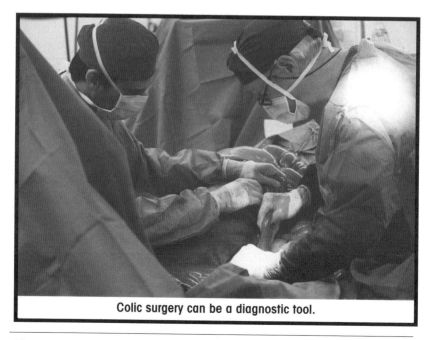

**Colic surgery can be a diagnostic tool.**

erwise move abdominal organs is severely restricted through the laparoscope. Therefore, a lesion that causes colic either could easily be missed or, even if it is identified, require a standard midline incisional approach to correct the problem. For this reason, surgical approaches to the abdomen must take into account the need to view the entire abdomen and manipulate abdominal organs, as well as to ascertain the requirements for correcting the problem. Often, laparoscopy may be used for biopsy of the intestines or other accessible organs or to access a lesion that diagnostic imaging has determined to be reachable. Exploratory midline incisional celiotomy can be used for all the things for which laparoscopy can be used but implies a much larger incision site, more expense, and much more time for complete recovery.

## BIOPSY

A biopsy of an organ or a mass is indicated if and when there is evidence of either persistent organ dysfunction and/or a non-infectious mass found either in association with an organ or lymph node or as a separate mass in the abdomen. The biopsy sample allows a certified pathologist to prepare and evaluate the tissue obtained by the biopsy under the microscope. This allows specific characterization of cell types of the tissue and of the inflammatory response (if one exists). Biopsy is used to diagnose tumors, some infections, immune-mediated disease, and other inflammatory conditions. It provides a specific diagnosis of the reason for organ dysfunction as the cause of colic, and permits more accurate prognosis and treatments to be shared with the owners. Biopsies should be performed only when clinically indicated and only after a clotting profile has been evaluated to assure adequate coagulation of blood. Bleeding can occur even with normal clotting profiles when kidney, liver, and other biopsies are performed.

The most commonly obtained biopsies from the horse abdomen include the liver, kidney, and rectum. Biopsy of the intestinal tract or other abdominal organs can be performed in numerous ways, depending on the organ(s) to be sampled and the target locations within the organ to be sampled. Small intestinal biopsy must be performed by surgical procedure using either the exploratory laparotomy or a laparoscopic approach. Lesions of the intestine sometimes can be seen throughout the intestinal tract. If this is the case, rectal biopsy may be performed in an attempt to characterize the generalized disease. Rectal biopsy can be performed in the standing and sedated patient, thereby avoiding the need for more invasive surgical approaches. However, rectal biopsies are low-yield procedures when the disease does not specifically involve the rectum. Large intestinal biopsies are less commonly obtained but also require one of the aforementioned surgical approaches. Biopsies of the liver are most often and easily performed in the standing sedated horse.

Liver biopsy is performed when there is a history of liver disease, blood chemistry findings indicative of liver dysfunction, abnormal ultrasound findings of the liver, and/or a mass identified in association with the liver. The liver biopsy is obtained directly through the body wall of the sedated horse. Kidney biopsies are commonly performed as well. They are obtained when there are indications of kidney dysfunction and/or there are abnormal findings of these organs by ultrasound examination. Kidney biopsies are also obtained through the body wall of the abdomen. Bleeding and hematoma formation are not uncommon after kidney biopsies. Less commonly, spleen and lymph nodes may be biopsied in the abdomen. Indications for such biopsy most often include masses of undetermined types in these structures. The organ or source of the mass may be difficult to interpret without biopsy. Abscesses in the abdomen or in association with an abdominal organ may best be left alone since leakage can cause contamination of the abdomen and a subsequent peritonitis. On occasion, aspiration and drainage of an abdominal abscess may be possible through a body wall to which it is adhered.

## SUMMARY OF THE DIAGNOSTICS

Naturally, not all of the above diagnostics are used in all cases of colic. The typical colic that presents as an emergency is generally first assessed for the level of pain and for the stability of the horse to determine the need for referral (surgical necessity or intense medical treatment for unstable cases), to provide palliative measures to control current and possible future abdominal pain, and to allot time for the horse to recover and resume normal intestinal function. Many of the diagnostics listed above (such as some of the more intensive imaging techniques, the carbohydrate absorption tests, endoscopic examinations of areas other than the esophagus, more specific blood testing and biopsies) are generally more often performed at referral hospitals for horses with chronic colic, weight loss, recurrent fever, and other signs of persistent illness.

# CHAPTER 3
## Major Conditions Associated with Colic

For most episodes of colic, a specific diagnosis is never reached because the abdominal pain resolves with minimal intervention. In fact, of all the episodes of colic pain that occur, an estimated 80% to 90% will resolve without significant intervention. Therefore, although the occurrence of colic is a significant concern, it does not mean every horse is destined for surgery or other intensive veterinary attention. Most colic episodes resolve relatively easily, even when veterinary attention is necessary (and a veterinary consultation is usually a good idea). The approach, as described earlier, is to perform some simple diagnostics and a physical examination, control the pain, control feed intake, and evaluate the response to therapy. With this initial approach, even horses that have been persistently uncomfortable often improve. The veterinarian usually cannot provide a specific diagnosis on the initial examination because he/she has not been able to evaluate the abdominal contents with anything other than perhaps a rectal examination, which permits blind evaluation of only a small portion of the abdomen. Therefore, if your veterinarian is not able to give a specific diagnosis for your horse's colic pain, do not be frustrated. The veterinarian is actually portraying the situation as it really exists.

The importance of veterinary attention for even the apparently mild cases of colic is severalfold: 1) to evaluate the health status of the horse, 2) to perform the physical examination and other diagnostics that may yield a specific diagno-sis, 3) to help control pain, 4) to assist the intestinal tract to return to normal physiologic function, and, perhaps most importantly, 5) to determine if the horse should be referred for further evaluation, treatment, and/or surgical intervention.

## COLIC ON THE FARM

Many horses that exhibit a colic episode on the farm (or otherwise outside of a hospital environment) may not ever have a specific diagnosis because they respond with minimal to moderate veterinary attention. Many of these horses may have become uncomfortable due to various intestinal upsets that can cause impaired or disorganized intestinal motility, intestinal gas accumulation, intestinal "clogging" of dry fecal material, or other temporary intestinal maladies or dysfunctions. These episodes may be similar to "cramping" or abdominal bloating (intestinal tympany) that occurs in people. They may induce significant discomfort for a period but are unlikely to require intensive intervention. In such situations passage of stool and/or gas can improve the situation. When your veterinarian comes to evaluate the horse, let him/her know if gas and/or stool has been passed.

On rare occasion a horse that colics cannot be transported for a surgical or medical referral (age, poor prognosis, finances, etc.). In such scenarios your farm veterinarian is your only reasonable hope of assessment, pain management, prognostication, and advice. It can be extremely difficult to know what to do in the face of severe abdominal pain. There cer-

### AT A GLANCE

- Between 80% and 90% of all colic episodes resolve without significant intervention.

- A veterinary examination is important for any suspected case of colic.

- Strangulating obstructions are the "worst-case scenario" of colic.

- Medical colic refers to any type of colic that does not require surgical intervention.

tainly are conditions that cause significant abdominal pain from which a horse may recover without surgery. However, prolonged pain and increasing instability of the horse are indications that recovery may not be feasible without more intensive intervention. Your regular veterinarian will help you make any necessary decisions for management and treatment of the colic. However, in the event of severe colic without other management and treatment alternatives, euthanasia may become a very real and very humane alternative for an owner to consider.

## SOME MAJOR CAUSES OF COLIC

### Impaction/Obstructive Colic (non-strangulating colic)

Impactions are simply accumulations of material within the intestinal tract that cause an obstruction and inhibit the passage of intestinal contents. Impactions may cause partial or complete intestinal non-strangulating obstruction anywhere they occur. The pain can range from very mild to violent, depending on the degree of obstruction and nature of the impaction. Intestinal non-strangulating obstructions may also occur by causes other than impactions. Feed material, foreign objects, parasites, intestinal displacements, enlargement or thickening of the intestinal wall, masses of any type, and intestinal strictures (sites of scarring that cause a narrowed intestinal lumen) can lead to non-strangulating obstruction of the intestine where they occur.

### Pelvic Flexure Impactions

One of the few causes of colic that can be specifically diagnosed on the farm, large intestinal impactions are relatively common. However, impactions, particularly pelvic flexure impactions, are probably overdiagnosed. In any colic episode or intestinal dysfunction, fecal material commonly accumulates in the large intestine, causing it to fill and to feel enlarged on a rectal examination. In such circumstance the accumulated fecal material may not really be the cause of the colic but rather a manifestation of altered intestinal function and motility. True impactions of the large intestine are extremely large and solid on rectal palpation. The most common site for large intestinal impactions to occur is at the pelvic flexure. This location makes an impaction relatively simple to diagnose because it is easily reached by rectal examination and often so extensive as to extend into the inlet of the pelvis. Horses with pelvic flexure impactions are most often treated medically, using intravenous fluids (often at hospitals), aggressive nasogastric intubation in association with the administration of mineral oil, magnesium sulfate, and occasionally dioctyl sodiumsulfosuccinate (DSS). These horses may be in significant pain. Therefore, pain management is particularly important. Horses should be kept from eating until the impaction is resolved. Drinking water is helpful, but many horses on intravenous fluids lose their "thirst" because they are receiving fluids in the vein. Horses with pelvic flexure impactions rarely require surgical intervention.

### Sand Impactions

In certain parts of the country, horses may accumulate sand in the large intestine over time. Sand is ingested while the horse eats hay or grass, and the sand "settles" in the large intestine (the colon). Horses with insufficient pasture or poor quality roughage may be more prone to accumulate sand while scavenging for forage. Sand tends to accumulate in the pelvic flexure, the ventral colon, and in the dorsal colon. Horses may develop watery stool from inflammation, or the sand may obstruct the intestinal flow. Sand may occasionally be seen on abdominal X-rays, but this technique requires specialized equipment and very high levels of radiation. Sand impaction seen on a radiograph must be distinguished from an enterolith (stone formation within the intestinal tract), which can look very similar on the film. Occasionally "sand colic" can be managed over time with daily administration of psyllium. However, psyllium therapy does not always completely remove significant amounts of sand nor prevent sand accumulation. Horses with repeat colic episodes or even acute colic may require surgical intervention and enterotomy (surgical opening of the stomach or intestine) to remove the sand from the large intestine. Horses in areas where there is a high sand content in the soil should be fed above the ground and provided high-quality forages free of sand.

### Cecal Impactions

Cecal impactions may be a sequel to previous abdominal or other surgeries, or to unrelated illness. Their incidence may be greater in horses with dental problems, poor forage in their diets, sand accumulation, limited access to water, heavy parasitism, hospitalization due to other illnesses, general anesthesia, and NSAID administration. The potential for rupture in addition to abdominal pain makes cecal impactions a cause for concern. For this reason cecal impactions are much more commonly approached surgically than are pelvic flexure impactions. Persistent pain is an indication for surgery. However, other clues used to determine the need for surgery include rectal examination findings pertaining to the cecum, analysis of abdominal fluid, and stability of the horse.

### Stomach Impaction

Stomach impactions are relatively uncommon and usually require surgery to diagnose. Affected horses may exhibit reflux through the nasogastric tube. The stomach cannot be palpated rectally, but ultrasound may provide a clue to the presence of gastric impaction. However, the definitive diagnosis is usually made during surgery. Stomach impactions may occur with feed obstructions, foreign bodies, motility disturbances, stomach outflow problems, or for no apparent reason. Non-surgical management of a stomach impaction is performed by passage of a nasogastric tube and stomach lavage using water with or without DSS, with intravenous fluids, and with other medications. Surgical approach is made if pain is persistent. Surgery allows manual decompression of the stomach and massage or mechanical breakdown and removal of stomach contents. Surgery also allows exploration of the remainder of the abdomen to evaluate for other intestinal conditions. In surgery, manual external massage of the stomach may suffice in relieving the impaction/obstruction. Enterotomy may be a problem for the surgeon since the stomach cannot be manipulated so that it is able to be lifted out from the abdomen. This substantially raises the risk of contamination of the abdomen with intestinal contents.

### Small Intestinal Impaction

Small intestinal impactions are more common in younger horses that have heavy parasite infestations (such as round worms, *Parascaris equorum*). Furthermore, younger horses may be more likely to exhibit pica and ingest foreign bodies such as bailing twine, plastic baggies, or other objects. These objects may lead to small intestinal obstructions if they fail to pass through the intestinal tract. Small intestinal obstructions and impactions may follow previous small intestinal surgery and anastomosis (connecting two relatively healthy segments of intestine), or may occur with a stricture (the narrowing of a passage), or a functional motility disturbance. Small intestinal obstructions of any type are frequently severe enough to warrant surgical intervention.

### Small Colon Impactions

Small colon impactions can be associated with foreign objects, dental problems, poor forage in the diet, poor hydration, parasitism, or motility disorders. The clinical signs may begin with mild colic pain but can progress to significant abdominal pain that may not respond to medical therapy. Initial medical therapy includes laxatives, intravenous fluids, and very careful administration of enemas. When medical therapy fails and/or the horse's condition deteriorates, surgery becomes necessary. Horses that have undergone small colon surgery and enterotomy may benefit from changes in feed to a complete pelleted diet to help minimize recurrence.

Farther down the intestinal tract, the rectum may also become impacted. However, the rectum can be evacuated manually without surgical intervention. Such impactions are relatively uncommon but may also benefit from careful administration of enemas, particularly in foals with meconium retention.

### Enteroliths

An enterolith is literally a "stone" that forms within the intestinal tract, almost exclusively in the large intestine. These intestinal stones form from the activity of various bacteria in combination with feeds. The stone typically forms around a nidus (anything that allows accumulation and hardening of material on it). The enterolith is usually composed of ammonium magnesium phosphate. Enteroliths in horses (termed enterolithiasis) seem to occur more often in certain areas of the country, particularly California. Horses with enteroliths may exhibit recurrent colic of various intensities. Most horses will exhibit obvious abdominal pain ranging from mild to severe and some will eat less. The colic examination is unlikely to provide any specific indication of an enterolith, making the horse a possible candidate for surgery if it exhibits the normal indications for surgery.

A chronic condition can cause intestinal damage and result in abnormal abdominal fluid. Intestinal rupture can occur secondary to enterolithiasis due to intestinal damage from the stone or intestinal obstruction. Abdominal radiography (X-rays) can help evaluate for the presence of an enterolith. This type of radiography requires very large X-ray machines and very intense techniques. Abdominal radiographs can reveal sand accumulation, which must be differentiated from an enterolith to facilitate proper treatment. Most often, enteroliths are discovered by exploratory abdominal surgery.

However, if an enterolith has been identified on a radiograph, the treatment is surgical removal by enterotomy and extrication from the intestinal lumen. Most enteroliths occur in the small colon or transverse colon but may be found elsewhere in the large intestine. Horses with enteroliths may have other intestinal abnormalities, including more than one enterolith.

## STRANGULATING OBSTRUCTIONS

If you are a horse owner, chances are you have heard horror stories about "colic" in horses. As we have already seen, there are many forms of colic, but strangulating obstructions are the colic cases that prompt these horror stories. A strangulating obstruction is a form of colic that the horse owner doesn't want. The term strangulating is used to describe what happens if and when the blood supply to the intestine and the flow of intestinal contents are partially or completely obstructed by some sort of twisting or other occlusion of the intestine itself and/or the mesenteric attachment that carries the blood supply to the intestine.

Strangulating obstructions are the "worst-case scenarios" for which veterinarians diligently try to evaluate during a colic episode. With intestinal and blood supply strangulation, the affected segment of intestine will quickly become deprived of oxygen, congested with blood that cannot return to the circulation, leading to the death of the affected segment of intestine. Therefore, time is of the essence and is the reason the examining veterinarian tries to determine whether the horse will require immediate transport, further evaluation, and possibly abdominal surgery. Owner input can greatly help the attending veterinarian, especially if the owner is willing to adopt the approach of "when in doubt, ship it out" — meaning don't wait for the need for surgery to become obvious before sending the horse to a surgical facility. Even if the horse becomes comfortable after or because of the trailer ride, no harm is done. At the surgical facility the horse can be closely monitored or taken directly to surgery if necessary.

Surgeons often use the term "volvulus" to describe an intestinal twist. Intestinal volvulus can occur nearly anywhere along the intestinal tract, so a very general distinction is made as to whether it occurs in the small intestine (small intestinal volvulus) or in the large intestine (large intestinal volvulus). Either location poses the danger of intestinal devitalization, loss of blood supply, and intestinal segmental death. Volvulus is an absolute surgical situation, and without surgery the horse is likely to experience a very painful and unpleasant death. Horses with a volvulus of any type are experiencing a severe cause of colic that rapidly leads to dehydration, pain, and poor stability due to shock. Deterioration can be extremely rapid. Indeed, volvulus tends to be the most violent type of colic, leading to rupture of the intestine and death.

How a horse fares after surgery depends on the factors previously outlined. However, the horse's chances are better the earlier surgery is performed. Intestinal strangulations will require a surgical resection (removal of unhealthy dead intestine) and an anastomosis. In some cases, the surgeon may determine that such procedures are unwarranted due to poor prognosis.

The surgeon will make a decision after diagnosing the problem at hand and assessing the appearance of the intestine, the stability of the patient under anesthesia, the ability to correct the problem, and the owner's wishes. Occasionally, the surgeon cannot remove all of the unhealthy intestine due to physical limitations imposed by the horse's anatomy. In such situations the surgeon must decide what amount of intestine he can take out or whether to discontinue surgery based on the horse's instability and prognosis for recovery. At this time, the surgeon must understand the owner's financial concerns. It can be expected that if compromises for surgical correction must be made during surgery for any reason (such as inability to access and remove all affected intestine), the recovery is likely to take longer, require much more intensive post-operative management, have an overall poorer prognosis, and be more expensive.

### Small Intestinal Volvulus

Small intestinal volvulus occurs when the small intestine (duodenum, jejunum, and ileum) become twisted along the mesenteric attachment to the intestine. Twisting of the intestine is often 360 degrees or greater. Small intestinal volvulus may occur as the primary cause of colic or may be secondary to a pre-existing condition. The length of intestine involved may be as little as a meter to nearly the entire length of the small intestine. Clinical signs of small intestinal volvulus include severe pain that responds poorly to pain management, rapidly deteriorating tissue perfusion, dehydration, and often copious amounts of fluid obtained from refluxing the stomach with a nasogastric tube (often more than 3 to 5 gallons). Rectal examination may reveal palpable loops of distended small intestine. Such a finding is abnormal because small intestine is not palpable in a normal horse. As horses with small intestinal volvulus become less stable, they also develop significant endotoxemia (as the intestine dies). Foals and yearlings may be more susceptible to this type of colic than adults.

### Large Colon Volvulus

Large intestinal volvulus (large colon volvulus) may also occur anywhere along the length of the colon. The incidence appears to be high in broodmares sometime shortly after foaling. The twisting that occurs typically is oriented in a clockwise direction as viewed from behind the horse. Large colon volvulus is not always strangulating. Non-strangulating volvulus may occur with twisting between 90 and 270 degrees. Abdominal pain is often initially mild to moderate but progresses to severe with duration and continued twisting. Abdominal distension may become apparent on examination of the animal and a rectal examination reveals multiple large loops of gas-distended large intestine. Clinical signs become more intense with strangulation and with twists between 270 and 360 degrees or more. With more severe twisting comes more intense pain. The horse destabilizes with poor tissue perfusion, high heart rate, endotoxemia, and devitalization of intestine with intestinal strangulation. As with small intestinal volvulus, strangulated large colon volvulus is an immediate surgical emergency.

### Strangulating Lipoma

Another cause of strangulating obstruction is a lipoma, a benign fatty tumor that can grow very large. Lipomas are relatively common in older horses and originate from the mesentery fat. As a lipoma grows, it develops a "stalk," such that the tumor is suspended like a pendulum within the abdomen. It can move about in the abdomen on the end of this 'stalk" that attaches the tumor to the mesentery. With longer stalks and the ability to move, the lipomas become increasingly able to wrap around intestine. Such an event can lead to occlusion of intestinal blood supply and to obstruction of the intestinal tract. Frequently, this occlusion is very tight and able to lead to acute colic and intestinal death of the affected segments.

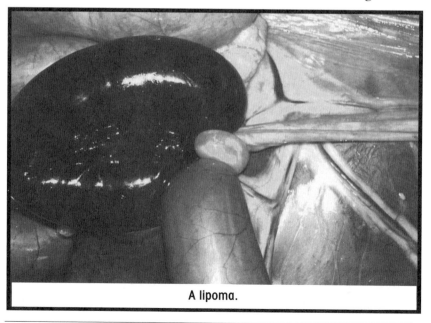

**A lipoma.**

When this type of strangulation occurs, the severity of the colic can be similar to that of a strangulating volvulus. Horses with strangulating lipomas face the same dangers because the effects of strangulation are the same for lipoma-induced strangulation — occluded blood supply and intestine that lead to tissue death of the affected segment of intestine, destabilization of the horse, and endotoxemia with potential for intestinal rupture. Surgery is necessary to reduce strangulation and remove the lipoma. Surgery often reveals other lipomas, which are usually removed at the same time if the horse's stability under general anesthesia will permit. Because this is also a strangulating lesion, a resection of intestine often is necessary. Because lipomas occur more commonly in older horses, intestinal resections may be harder on the affected horse and require more intensive post-operative therapy. Depending on the appearance and viability of the intestine, the patient's stability, and the amount of intestine that requires resection, euthanasia might be a prudent option for some older horses.

### Epiploic Foramen Entrapment

One particular type of strangulating intestinal disorder is related to a displacement of small intestine through a small hole or foramen, the borders of which are made up by the liver, pancreas, and two large veins (the vena cava and the hepatic portal vein). In most horses this foramen is rather small. This intestinal abnormality is referred to as an epiploic foramen entrapment. As a horse ages or develops liver disease, the foramen may enlarge slightly. A piece of small intestine (most often the ileum) may enter this normally small foramen and become obstructed. On occasion the result is a simple obstruction of small intestine without blood supply compromise. However, more commonly the obstruction is strangulating and involves both the ileum and the jejunum (both segments of small intestine). Horses with epiploic foramen entrapment often exhibit severe pain. Surgical correction is necessary but not easily performed because the foramen is in an anatomically disadvantageous location and the affected intestine is often very delicate. Furthermore, the structures, especially the nearby veins, are also very delicate and tearing of one of these will result in rapid death. Epiploic foramen entrapment cannot usually be distinguished without exploratory surgery. The clinical presentation is nearly identical to that of small intestinal strangulation due to volvulus or other small intestinal strangulating obstructions.

## CONDITIONS THAT MAY BE EITHER STRANGULATING OR NON-STRANGULATING

### Intussusception

An intussusception is an abnormal condition that occurs when one segment of intestine "telescopes" into an adjacent segment of intestine. To visualize this, consider a ship captain's hand-held telescope that folds into itself or collapses when the instrument is compressed at the ends. Such is the situation with intussusceptions. There are two pieces of intestinal segments that are referred to in describing the intussusception. The first piece is called the intussusceptum and does the telescoping into the attached segment. The second segment, referred to as the intussuscipiens, is attached to the first but must be larger in diameter to "receive" the telescoping intussusceptum. The length of intestine involved in the intussusception may vary greatly, and the condition can occur in either the small or large intestine. Colic due to an intussusception may recur due to partial obstruction. In fact, the "telescoping" can occur intermittently, correct, and recur again. However, many intussusceptions remain in the abnormal position. With time the affected intestine may become highly inflamed and irritated and the "telescoped" piece, the intussusceptum, may become blood- and oxygen-deprived and eventually die.

### Small Intestinal Intussusception

Intussusception of the small intestine may occur at nearly

any site. However, intussusception of the small intestine involving relatively shorter segments is often associated with the ileum in which the ileum telescopes into itself (ileoileal intussusception). Ileoileal intussusceptions may cause only partial obstructions and recurrent colic. Longer segments are involved in intussusceptions of the jejunum and the ileum and more commonly cause complete obstruction of the intestine. Intussusception of the ileum (small intestine) into the cecum (large intestine) is probably one of the most common types of intussusception. Ileocecal intussusception generally also leads to complete obstruction of the intestine. Strangulation with any intussusception may lead to persistent inflammation and pressure/stricture at the site where the invagination intussusceptum telescopes into the intussuscipiens. Surgical correction, resection of affected intestine, and anastomosis are generally required for both strangulating and for non-strangulating intussusception. Risk factors for intussusceptions include intestinal inflammation (enteritis) and motility dysfunction, heavy ascarid infestations (roundworms), tapeworm infestation (*Anoplocephala*), dietary changes, and some medications that alter intestinal motility.

### Large Intestinal Intussusception

Most large intestinal intussusceptions involve the cecum. These include cecocecal (cecum telescoping into itself) and cecocolic (cecum telescopes into the colon) intussusceptions. Such intussusceptions are reported to occur more frequently in younger horses (three years and younger), but the condition also affects older horses. Specific causes of such intussusceptions are generally unclear. However, abnormal intestinal motility between the involved segments of intestine likely plays a role. Risk factors for the development of large intestinal intussusception are generally the same as those described for small intestinal intussusception. In particular, tapeworms have been strongly associated with cecocecal and cecocolic intussusceptions, identified in 50% to 80% of these types of large intestinal intussusceptions. Other types of large intestinal intussusception are possible (colon telescoping into itself) but appear to be relatively uncommon. Clinical signs of horses with large intestinal intussusception vary. Acute forms may present with severe abdominal pain. However, chronic colic with reduced fecal output, weight loss, and intermittent fever may also be the presenting complaints. As with any other cause of colic, horses that develop compromised blood supply to the intestine may begin to demonstrate signs of shock, endotoxemia, and peritonitis (inflammation of the abdominal cavity — see Medical Conditions Associated with Chronic Colic). Surgical correction requires resection of affected intestine and anastomosis of similar portions of intestine or complete removal of the cecum to re-establish a functional large intestine. Horses with large intestinal intussusception generally have a guarded prognosis that at least partially depends on the segments affected, the amount of intestine involved, and the presence and severity of peritonitis.

## HERNIAS

An intestinal hernia is defined as a condition in which a segment of intestine protrudes through a normal or an abnormal hole in a wall of the cavity within which the segment of intestine normally exists. The most commonly encountered hernias in horses include epiploic foramen entrapment (see Strangulating Obstructions), internal herniation, inguinal and scrotal hernias, umbilical hernias, and diaphragmatic hernias. Each has the potential to cause colic in the horse.

### Internal Herniation

Internal herniation occurs when small intestine becomes trapped within a normal or an abnormal opening in the abdominal cavity. Technically speaking, epiploic foramen entrapment is a form of internal herniation in which a segment of small intestine is trapped in the epiploic foramen. Other openings in the abdominal cavity that can trap herniated intestine include the nephrosplenic space, tears or defects in the mesentery, the omentum, the gastrosplenic ligament, and the broad ligament. The gastrosplenic ligament exists between the stomach and the spleen. Small intestine may herniate through tears in this ligament and lead to strangulation.

Abnormal bands of fibrous adhesions and congenital abnormalities may also form spaces in the abdomen through which intestine may herniate. A band called a mesodiverticular band develops from an artery supplying the yolk of the embryo (vitilline artery) and its associated mesentery. It may fail to atrophy during development. The band is commonly then found in the lower portion of the jejunum (small intestine) and extends from one side of the mesentery to another, creating a triangular space capable of entrapping intestine. Another developmental aberration is called a Meckel's diverticulum. This structure is a remnant of the duct that connects the yolk of the embryo to the embryonic intestinal tract. Meckel's diverticulum forms a blind extension from the surface of the jejunum or ileum (small intestine). On occasion, a fibrous band runs from the top of this diverticulum to the umbilicus. The diverticulum can become impacted and die, leading to rupture. It can also entangle and strangulate small intestine or form an axis for a volvulus.

### Inguinal/Scrotal Hernias

Herniation of intestine may also occur into the inguinal canal through which the blood supply and "plumbing" for the male reproductive structures travel on their way to the testicles and scrotum. Females also have inguinal rings but without the extra tissue found in males. Perhaps because of their smaller ring, inguinal hernias are seldom found in fillies, and in foals the problem seldom causes intestinal obstruction. When a hernia does occur, which is more likely in a stallion but still relatively uncommon, it may become strangulating and require surgery. On occasion, non-strangulating inguinal hernias may also require surgery.

Scrotal hernias only occur in males. Scrotal herniation is a consideration in any case of acute colic in intact males. Scrotal herniation is really a more advanced type of inguinal hernia because the small intestine must pass through the inguinal canal to herniate into the scrotum. Such herniation may or may not be strangulating and require surgical intervention. Often the intestine can be palpated in the scrotum of the intact male or become obvious on ultrasound examination.

### Umbilical Hernias

Umbilical hernias occur in foals and are seldom strangulating. Most often a small portion of the small intestine (ileum) may become trapped through a small defect in the foal's body wall. The hernia is often manually reducible but occasionally requires an apparatus to hold the intestine in the abdomen so the body wall can close over. The apparatus, which your veterinarian can make, may be a hernia clamp or something more simple such as Elasticon® tape and a half of a tennis ball placed over the site.

### Diaphragmatic Hernia

Diaphragmatic herniation occurs when a segment of intestine herniates through the diaphragm. The intestine that herniates is usually small intestine but can also be large intestine if the tear in the diaphragm is large enough. When this occurs, strangulation of the involved segment of intestine often results. Tears in the diaphragm may be congenital (present at birth) or secondary to trauma or some other event, such as foaling or a fall over an obstacle. When large intestine is involved in the diaphragmatic hernia, the horse may exhibit respiratory difficulty. Rectal examination and diagnostic imaging can diagnose the condition. The modalities commonly employed for imaging include ultrasound and/or radiography of the chest. Surgery is necessary to remove the intestine from the chest, place it back into a correct position, and close the tear in the diaphragm. This surgery can be technically difficult to perform.

### Thromboembolic Colic

This type of colic is also referred to as non-strangulating intestinal infarction, meaning the area of affected intestine has experienced vascular compromise for reasons other than mechanical twisting and occlusion. The triggering event is associated with vascular disease or perhaps even a "clot" that has led to reduced blood supply or complete loss of blood supply to the affected intestine. This condition has been associated with inflammation of the cranial mesenteric artery due to larval migration of large strongyles (infant stages of intestinal worms). However, the condition may also be seen with other problems related to poor blood flow such as shock and intestinal distension. Pain that occurs with this type of colic may vary from mild to severe. Prolonged loss of blood supply to the affected intestine can lead to death of the affected intestine and significant leakage of intestinal contents into the abdomen with eventual rupture. Mild forms may respond to therapy without surgery. However, when significant blood flow and intestinal compromise are present, surgery may become necessary. Intestinal resection and anastomosis are likely to be required if this type of colic reaches such severity.

## INTESTINAL DISPLACEMENTS

Most intestinal displacements that lead to colic are associated with the large intestine. A large colon volvulus also can be regarded as an intestinal displacement. This condition was addressed earlier. As mentioned, strangulation becomes likely when the volvulus is 270 degrees or more. Other relatively common displacements are described by the direction in which the large intestine is displaced.

### Left Dorsal Displacement of the Colon (Nephrosplenic Entrapment)

Left dorsal displacement of the colon (LDDC) is also referred to as nephrosplenic entrapment of the large colon. As the name implies, the condition is associated with the entrapment of the left colon in a space between the kidney and the spleen where it may literally "hang" over the ligament between these two organs (on the left side of the abdomen as viewed from behind the horse). The movement necessary to cause this leads to displacement of the involved segment of large intestine laterally (to the left) and dorsally (towards the back) in the abdomen. Intestinal strangulation with this condition is rare. However, intestinal obstruction may occur when the flow of the intestinal contents is occluded by the weight of the large intestine that becomes "draped" over the nephrosplenic ligament (between the kidney and the spleen). The condition causes variable intensity of pain and is probably caused by the build up of gas and distension of the large intestine. More severe cases may exhibit unrelenting severe abdominal pain. A diagnosis is often made by a combination of rectal examination findings, ultrasound examination of the left flank of the horse that fails to image the left kidney due to the overlying large intestine, and surgical exploration. This type of colic may initially be addressed by medical therapy and physical external manipulations. Administration of the drug phenylephrine and subsequent forced exercise are thought occasionally to correct the entrapment. Phenylephrine induces contraction of the equine spleen. The contraction may help the colon "fall out" of the nephrosplenic space alone or in combination with exercise. If this fails, some hospitals may choose to "roll" the horse.

This procedure is also performed externally but requires that the horse be anesthetized and then placed into recumbency with the right side down. Hobbles are attached to the hind limbs, and the horse is lifted onto its back by a mechanical hoist. The abdomen is rocked back and forth in this position, and the hind end is lowered to place the horse into recumbency with its left side down. A rectal and/or ultrasound evaluation is performed to evaluate for correction of the entrapment. The procedure may be repeated and can also be performed in conjunction with the administration of phenylephrine. However, non-surgical manipulations and medical therapies for this condition are probably only successful about 50% of the time. If correction cannot be confirmed using rectal examination and ultrasonography, the horse is immediately taken to surgery for exploration and correction of the problem. With uncomplicated neprosplenic entrapments, surgery is easily performed with a good prognosis. Some horses have recurring nephrosplenic entrapment. Surgical procedures to prevent recurrence exist but should only be considered if a horse has experienced more than one episode.

### Right Dorsal Displacement of the Colon

Displacement of the large colon may also occur toward the right side of the abdomen (as viewed from behind the horse). Displacement of the large colon occurs between the cecum and the right body wall. Occasionally, the displacement is accompanied by a volvulus of the large colon. The volvulus may be either strangulating or non-strangulating in nature. Clinical signs of right dorsal displacement of the colon vary highly. Prolonged recurrent or chronic colic may be the primary clinical sign, or the presentation may be severe and acute. Diagnosis and the correction most often require exploratory surgery. Rectal examination findings tend to be relatively non-specific with large colon gas distension and perhaps indications of "out of place" large intestine.

## COLIC IN THE PREGNANT MARE

### Uterine Torsion

Torsion of the uterus occurs in the pregnant mare and often in the last trimester. Torsion occurs from 180 to 540 degrees in either direction. The cause appears to be fetal activity and movement and/or rolling by the mare. Clinical signs include persistent or recurrent colic. Mares usually continue to pass feces unless a segment of intestine has become compromised along with the uterine twist. The severity of the pain appears to be directly related to the degree of torsion, but mares with intestine entrapped with the twist experience severe pain. On occasion mares may develop uterine torsion at term, and dystocia occurs with the twisted uterine body that prevents normal delivery by closing off the birth canal.

A diagnosis of uterine torsion is made by rectal examination because the twist cannot usually be palpated through the vagina. On occasion a segment of small colon may become constricted as a result of the uterine twist and may obstruct the examiner's ability to perform a full rectal examination. The foal may become distressed by the uterine torsion due to compromised blood supply to the uterus, develop severe problems, and die in utero. The uterus itself may become severely compromised due to lack of blood supply. It may become necrotic and eventually rupture. Therefore, a quick diagnosis is imperative for both the mare and foal so that immediate steps can be taken to correct the torsion.

Corrective approaches include rolling the mare, standing surgery through the flank, general anesthesia and abdominal surgery through the ventral midline, and, in certain circumstances, manual rotation of the foal and the uterus through the cervix. Many clinicians prefer to correct the uterine torsion through standing flank surgery if the mare is tolerant and the uterus has not ruptured. If the uterus is corrected and the foal is dead, the mare usually aborts the fetus naturally after the surgery. If the foal is alive and has not been compromised, the pregnancy may progress normally after surgical correction. Less severely twisted and compromised uterine torsions may be approached non-surgically by administering general anesthesia to the mare and rolling her to untwist the uterus. Depending on the technique used, a plank might be placed across the abdomen to hold the uterus in place while the horse is rotated (rolled) around the uterus. Although this technique is very successful in cows, the "plank in the flank" technique is less effective in horses.

Mares that are in the process of foaling and have a uterine torsion are often presented for dystocia. When the twist is less than 270 degrees, it may be possible to correct the torsion through the cervix. Use of an epidural anesthetic or general anesthesia and a hoist may facilitate manipulation through the cervix. If the twist is greater than 270 degrees and the viability of the foal and/or uterus warrants rapid intervention, general anesthesia and a ventral midline approach may be indicated. When this occurs, an emergency team should be standing by with appropriate medications and equipment to resuscitate and support the foal as soon as it is delivered. Potential complications following uterine torsion include tearing of the uterus, peritonitis, and premature placental separation and death of the foal.

### Uterine Rupture

Rupture of the uterus at or near foaling can lead to peritonitis and colic. Diagnosis is made by rectal and uterine examination, ultrasound examination, abdominal fluid evaluation, and exploratory abdominal surgery. Surgery is indicated for repair of the uterine rupture; however, a small tear can receive conservative treatment of antibiotics and anti-inflammatory agents. Intravenous fluid therapy, peritoneal lavage/drainage, and plasma therapy may also be required with medical treatment. Prognosis is poor with gross contamination of the abdomen.

### Uterine Artery Rupture

Occasionally, mares eleven years and older may exhibit colic during or shortly after foaling in association with an acute rupture or bleed from a uterine artery. Fatal bleeding is most often encountered in mares greater than 18 years of age. The cause is believed to be age-related degeneration of the arterial wall. This artery is most often the middle uterine artery but may be the utero-ovarian artery or the external iliac artery. Bleeding is initiated by the additional stress of pregnancy on the broad ligament and arteries supplying the uterus from increased arterial pressures and direct pressure during foaling. Bleeding leads to the formation of a hematoma within the broad ligament of the uterus. Colic occurs due to the stretching of the ligament and associated structures from the presence of the hematoma. Bleeding stops when the hematoma effectively clots, but the broad ligament may also rupture under the stretching of the ligament. This can lead to rapid and severe hemorrhage into the abdomen and rapid death due to acute blood loss. A rupture of the external iliac artery leads to rapid death because the artery is not housed in any ligament that can assist in clot formation. Bleeding occurs rapidly and directly into the abdomen and leads to rapid death after rupture.

Clinical signs of uterine artery rupture may include colic, sweating, increased heart and respiratory rates, pale membranes, depression, weakness, and collapse. Diagnosis is made by clinical signs, rectal palpation of a hematoma in the broad ligament, and ultrasound examination. Abdominal fluid evaluation may reveal fresh blood in the abdomen. Evaluation of the red blood cell parameters are compatible with blood loss anemia but may be unapparent for up to 24 hours. Less severe or mild bleeds may be undetected for some time. Some mares are treated for colic until a rectal examination after foaling reveals a hematoma.

Cases of severe or uninhibited bleeding can lead to death. Surgical intervention to ligate (to "tie off" with suture) the bleeding artery is unlikely to succeed due to poor surgical access to the area and the patient's instability and intolerance of general anesthesia. Treatment of horses with uterine artery bleeds often includes therapy for shock due to blood loss. This includes ensuring cardiac output and tissue perfusion. Despite significant blood loss, fluids must be used with caution because volume expansion using fluids can lead to increased blood pressure and renewed bleeding.

Conservative management of uterine artery rupture includes minimizing stress and excitement and administering acepromazine to help reduce mean arterial pressure. Naloxone has been reported to be helpful in some mares with uterine artery rupture. Pain medications are often necessary to control colic. Blood volume replenishment using whole blood or intravenous fluids is often indicated to help preserve cardiac output. Aggressive therapy involves use of all available treatments and aggressive volume expansion with close monitoring of pressures and tissue perfusion.

Other medications that may be used include aminocaproic acid, 10% formalin, anti-inflammatory agents, pentoxifylline, intranasal oxygen, and a belly wrap for external pressure. The prognosis for mares with uterine artery rupture is guarded. Mares that survive the initial crisis must be kept quiet for several weeks to permit the clot to resolve and the vessel to heal. Complete healing of the vessel injury may take up to several months. Mares that survive uterine artery rupture are at significantly high risk for recurrence with subsequent pregnancy and foaling. They should, therefore, not be rebred. Mares that have no value other than as broodmares must only be rebred when the hematoma has fully resolved. Appropriate preparations for the foal must be made in case the mare dies during subsequent foaling. Prevention for any mare that has experienced a previous uterine artery rupture includes avoidance of heavy exercise and stressful situations.

## MEDICAL CONDITIONS THAT CAUSE COLIC

Medical colic refers to any cause of colic that does not require surgical intervention. These types of colic are treated by medical therapy such as medications, dietary modifications, and nasogastric administration of lubricants or laxatives. Such conditions are primarily associated with intestinal or other organ dysfunction not necessarily associated with a physical abnormality of the organ. Medical colic is, however, associated with physiological dysfunction of the intestine or obstruction of the intestine with feed or fecal material.

Impactions are generally regarded as medical colics, particularly those affecting the pelvic flexure of the large intestine. This is because pelvic flexure impactions rarely require surgical intervention. Other impactions may be more commonly associated with surgery, such as small intestinal or cecal impactions. They may be managed initially as medical colic but may require surgical intervention if medical treatment does not lead to prompt resolution of the problem.

## ACUTE NON-SURGICAL (MEDICAL) COLIC THAT MAY REQUIRE REFERRAL

### Enteritis

Enteritis is a non-specific term used to describe any inflammatory condition of the intestine. Enteritis occurs with many intestinal conditions that cause colic and is present if and when the intestine has been manipulated and/or surgically incised following colic surgery. However, enteritis may also be present in the intestine without any specific physical abnormality and can actually be a cause of a colic episode. Enteritis may be a result of an infectious agent in the intestinal tract or a sequel to an obstruction or motility disturbance. Therefore, enteritis may be a diagnosis in some horses with colic. It is still relatively unclear what leads to all cases of enteritis as the cause of colic, but certain bacteria such as various species of *Salmonella* or *Clostridia* are often implicated. Other potential causes may include viruses, *Ehrlichia risticii* (Potomac Horse Fever), sand, parasites, and some medications. Enteritis may be acute or chronic in nature. The chronic inflammatory conditions of the intestine are discussed in the section on Chronic Colic.

### Large Intestinal Enteritis (Diarrhea/colitis)

Enteritis that affects the large intestine is often referred to as colitis, is commonly associated with diarrhea, and has numerous potential causes. Diarrhea is most often addressed with supportive care and dietary management. Supportive care may require intensive management in severe cases of colitis. If diarrhea is profuse, large volumes of intravenous fluids are often required because horses can become severely dehydrated. Horses that become dehydrated must be medically managed carefully by avoiding drugs that are highly toxic to the kidneys during states of dehydration. These include aminoglycoside antibiotics (such as gentamicin) and nonsteroidal anti-inflammatory drugs (such as phenylbutazone). Access to fresh water and/or water with electrolytes may also help replenish ongoing fluid losses. Horses that lose fluids in the stool also tend to lose a lot of electrolytes. Therefore, intravenous and oral fluids are often supplemented with extra electrolytes such as calcium, potassium, and chloride. Furthermore, horses with diarrhea and colitis tend to lose large volumes of protein from the blood into the intestine. This protein is then passed in the stool. The situation may become so severe that it becomes difficult to keep fluid in the vascular space (due to the loss of osmotic draw that protein in the blood provides). This can lead to the development of severe edema in the limbs and along the abdomen. Such situations are often addressed by the administration of plasma (rich in blood proteins) and/or other synthetic colloid fluids such as hetastarch or Oxyglobin®.

Colic is common with large intestinal enteritis as a result of gas and fluid distension and significant motility disturbances. Horses with colitis often develop fevers and signs of endotoxemia (see section on Endotoxemia) due to absorption of toxins from the intestinal tract in association with significant physiological disturbances of normal intestinal functions. Other major concerns with diarrhea and endotoxemia are the development of laminitis and peritonitis. Anti-endotoxic and/or anti-laminitic therapies are often administered in addition to fluid and protein administration. Antibiotics are often not administered unless the endotoxemia has led to a low white cell count, possibly making the horse more susceptible to infections. Anytime a horse develops diarrhea, there is the potential for a life-threatening situation. For this reason, any horse with diarrhea should be carefully examined and managed by a veterinarian.

The most common infectious concerns for large intestinal enteritis (colitis) include *Salmonella spp*, *Clostridia spp*, and *Ehrlichia risticii* (Potomac Horse Fever) in adults, and *Escherichia coli*, rotavirus, *Salmonella spp*, and *Rhodococcus equi* in foals. Specific antibiotic therapies are generally not applicable for most infectious diarrheas. In fact, antibiotic administration may be a factor capable of inducing diarrhea in many horses. Antibiotics such as trimethoprim/sulfa, ceftiofur, oxytetracycline, and erythromycin are regarded as agents commonly associated with diarrhea. However, nearly any antibiotic has the potential to cause diarrhea and colitis in the horse. The primary mechanism of this is the killing of a "normal population" of enteric bacteria. Their death allows more pathogenic strains of bacteria to colonize the large intestine, leading to pathologic disruption of normal intestinal function. For Potomac Horse Fever specifically, oxytetracycline is considered to be a specific antibiotic for the treatment and elimination of *Ehrlichia risticii*. Appropriate use of oxytetracycline for Potomac Horse Fever often produces significant improvement in clinical signs and cessation of diarrhea after only a few treatments. The diagnosis of Potomac Horse Fever, however, can be difficult and oxytetracycline may not help and may even worsen diarrhea and colitis if the diarrhea is due to another cause. Metronidazole is an antibiotic that is specifically used to treat diarrhea due to *Clostridia spp*.

Other medications associated with the development of colitis are the non-steroidal anti-inflammatory drugs (NSAIDs — phenylbutazone, flunixin meglumine, ketoprofen, etc.). These medications, with chronic usage or individual susceptibilities, may cause ulceration not only of the stomach and small intestine but also of the large intestine. Such ulceration often occurs in the right dorsal colon; thus, the syndrome that affects the large intestine due to these medications is often referred to as "right dorsal colitis." The condition may or may not be associated with diarrhea; however, it commonly causes colic and weight loss in the horse. The diagnosis of right dorsal colitis is often made by exclusion of other causes of colitis, and when the horse exhibits weight loss with ultrasound examination of the right dorsal colon, and exploratory surgery with biopsy of the right dorsal colon. The history may include the administration of non-steroidal anti-inflammatory drugs. Management of cases of right dorsal colitis involves changing the diet to low-bulk feeds, avoiding all non-steroidal anti-inflammatory drugs, minimizing stress, and administering anti-ulcer therapy and/or the drug sucralfate. In some instances other medications may be used such as metronidazole (an antibiotic). Metronidazole is used not for its antibiotic effects in right dorsal colitis cases but rather for some proposed anti-inflammatory effects. Psyllium mucilloid may also be used continuously to generate short-chain fatty acids that could help repair the lining (mucosa) of the colon. Misoprostil® has been suggested for use in the management of ulceration anywhere in the intestinal tract and to help prevent ulceration due to non-steroidal anti-inflammatory drugs. It may be particularly useful in further medical management of right dorsal colitis. Right dorsal colitis is included in this book under sections on Enteritis and Ulcers because it causes both of these conditions simultaneously.

### Small Intestinal Enteritis (Anterior Enteritis, Duodenitis-proximal Jejunitis)

Commonly referred to as anterior enteritis, small intestinal enteritis describes the inflammation and physiological dysfunction of the small intestine without any associated physical obstruction or twist. The correct term for this condition, duodenitis-proximal jejunitis (DPJ), describes the most common specific location of the inflammatory process, which is the duodenum and the segment of the jejunum just "downstream" from the duodenum. The result of this inflammation is often severe reduction in motility of the small intestine and accumulation of fluid in the intestine that cannot move through the intestinal tract. The inflammatory process of the small intestine leads to additional fluid and protein loss from the vascular space (blood) into the intestine, which exacerbates the accumulation of intestinal fluid already occurring. Horses may become severely dehydrated and develop poor perfusion of the other tissues. Because the rate of accumulation of this fluid in the intestine overwhelms the rate that it is passed down the intestinal tract, the fluid begins to back up in the small intestine and into the stomach. The fluid may eventually reflux spontaneously (when pressures become high) through the esophagus and out the nose. With continual pressure accumulation and inflammation, the stomach is in danger of rupture. Horses with significant intestinal fluid and gas accumulation can develop severe pain. This pain is often greatly reduced by veterinary attention and by passage of a nasogastric tube to relieve the stomach and small intestine of the accumulated gas, fluid, and pressure. Horses with anterior enteritis often produce this fluid and gas rapidly at the expense of the fluid volume in the blood. Because of this tendency a nasogastric tube is often left in to provide a continuous "pop-off" valve to relieve pressure and fluid.

Horses with anterior enteritis are most often managed medically (without surgery). However, it can be very difficult to distinguish anterior enteritis from a strangulating or obstructing lesion of the small intestine that requires surgical attention. Rectal examination does not help to distinguish anterior enteritis from other forms of small intestinal colic. Horses with anterior enteritis often become much more comfortable after removing excess fluid and gas off the stomach. This is often manifest by either temporary resolution of the clinical signs of abdominal pain and/or by significant reduction in the heart rate.

Furthermore, a number of horses with anterior enteritis have fevers that support this purely inflammatory condition. However, not all of the cases of anterior enteritis follow these generalizations, and any time a horse has persistent pain, consideration of surgical intervention is warranted. For this reason a number of horses with anterior enteritis undergo exploratory abdominal surgery. This is appropriate because if the condition is not anterior enteritis, it may be a surgical problem that requires quick intervention to prevent strangulation and death of a segment of intestine, to reduce the likelihood of the need for a surgical resection and anastomosis, and to maximize the potential for a successful outcome. Furthermore, a number of surgeons and internists believe that some horses with anterior enteritis may benefit from surgical decompression and stripping of fluid from the small intestine.

Medical management of horses with anterior enteritis involves intense care. These horses are given intravenous fluids at high flow rates and are refluxed frequently, often every two hours. Without intravenous fluids these horses will quickly become dehydrated. Horses that become dehydrated must be medically managed carefully by avoiding drugs that are highly toxic to the kidneys. Intravenous antibiotics are not always administered. However, some clinicians believe there is a significant association of anterior enteritis and clostridial bacteria. Therefore, penicillin may be used to treat for any potentially pathogenic clostridium species. Other antibiotics may be added if endotoxemia develops and suppresses the white cell count, making the horse more susceptible to infections. Endotoxemia is common in horses with anterior enteritis. Because of this horses with this condition are at risk of developing laminitis. Anti-endotoxic therapies are often employed with or without the addition of anti-laminitic therapies. Horses with anterior enteritis may reflux for a week to 10 days or more, while others may reflux only for a day. In uncomplicated cases the prognosis is usually good, but the expenses for management can be significant.

### Impactions of the Pelvic Flexure

This type of colic has been addressed under the section on Impaction Colic. It is presented here because this condition is almost always treated by medical therapy (non-surgical). The physical examination findings are non-specific, and pain exhibited is often mild to moderate but may become severe. The rectal examination usually determines the impaction and its location, and nasogastric intubation produces no reflux. Management of the condition involves pain control and super-hydration to facilitate break up of the impacted fecal material. Intravenous fluids are often administered in the hospital. Horses are usually "tubed" with water and some laxative or lubricating agents such as magnesium sulfate and mineral oil. Some clinicians prefer to use DSS (dioctyl sodiumsulfosuccinate) to help resolve the impaction, but this substance can significantly irritate the lining (mucosa) of the intestinal tract. As the impaction begins to break down, pain reduces in intensity and frequency of fecal production increases. The fecal material may be watery when passed. On occasion, the passage of feces may be explosive. Overall prognosis of this condition with appropriate management is good to excellent.

### Ulcers

Intestinal ulceration is a relatively common problem in horses, particularly in performance horses. Gastric (stomach), duodenal (small intestine), and colonic (large intestine) ulcers all occur. Horses in performance situations or in stressful environments, such as overcrowding, and horses that receive non-steroidal anti-inflammatory drugs are all predisposed to the development of intestinal ulceration in any location. Certain feeding practices, such as high-concentrate, low-forage diets, may predispose to the development of ulcers (see Introduction). Various investigations of the prevalence of stomach ulcers have revealed that most performance horses do harbor gastric ulcers. The prevalence may increase with intensity of competition and training and with stress associated with competition. Such stress might include frequent shipping, lack of access to pasture, feeding of highly caloric or starchy diets, and exposure to transmissible diseases.

Although many horses do harbor gastric ulcers, the clinical signs of their presence may vary greatly. (Ulcers that cause colic in one horse may cause no obvious clinical signs in another.) Furthermore, some clinical signs of ulcers are relatively ambiguous. Performance horses may exhibit only a dull coat and prolonged time to complete their feed. Other horses may exhibit overt signs of recurrent colic and weight loss. Horses may lose protein and blood in the feces in association with intestinal ulceration. A diagnosis of gastric ulceration is made by endoscopic examination of the stomach after an overnight fast. Gastroscopic examination of the stomach requires specialized equipment and clinical expertise in the procedure. Although the presence of ulcers in the stomach may be apparent, their clinical significance may be difficult to interpret. This may require an evaluation of the response to treatment of the ulcers. Duodenal ulcers are difficult to visualize, even with an endoscope. They may be more common in younger horses and foals, where they may be severe and life-threatening. Severe stomach and duodenal ulcers in foals can rupture and lead to acute death of the foal. It is occasionally possible to visualize duodenal ulcers in foals endoscopically. Response to treatment usually serves as the key to interpreting the presence of ulcers in the duodenum, but often ulcers in the stomach and duodenum co-exist in young horses. Foals are often treated for ulcers prophylactically in hospital environments or other stressful environments due to their potentially severe consequences. Ulcers that exist in the colon are usually diagnosed presumptively and by exclusion of other intestinal problems that cause chronic colic, weight loss, and possibly loss of protein in the intestinal tract.

Evaluation of the large intestine for ulcers may focus on the right dorsal colon and the syndrome of right dorsal colitis previously described. The condition is often highly associated with the administration of non-steroidal anti-inflammatory drugs for an extended time.

Treatment of ulcers involves medical therapy that serves to reduce acid production in the stomach. Medications commonly used in horses include cimetidine, ranitidine, and omeprazole. Cimetidine and ranitidine are known as H2 blockers that indirectly reduce acid production. They are generally much less effective in the treatment of gastric ulcers than the drug omeprazole. Omeprazole directly inhibits acid secretion in the stomach and has been shown to be highly effective in treating severe gastric ulceration. Ranitidine may help prevent stomach ulceration once a therapeutic course of omeprazole has completely resolved active stomach ulceration. Sucralfate is much like a Band-Aid to the stomach lining by binding to ulcerated sites and serving partially as a protective barrier from the stomach acid environment. It does not reduce acidity of the stomach. It has been used for foals with stomach ulcers but is now often replaced by omeprazole for prevention. Misoprostil® has been suggested for use in the management of ulceration anywhere in the intestinal tract, and it may help prevent ulceration due to non-steroidal anti-inflammatory drugs. It also may be particularly useful in medical management of right dorsal colitis. Even when the ulceration involves more than the right dorsal colon, the management of the condition is similar to that of right dorsal colitis, which is covered in the section on Large Intestinal Enteritis.

### Gastric Outflow Obstruction

As a sequel to inflammation, erosion, and ulceration of the pylorus of the stomach and of the duodenum, the normal emptying of the stomach may be impaired. This can occur by disruption of coordinated nervous system activity or by scarring of the pylorus (the outflow segment of the stomach that leads directly into the small intestine) or duodenum that causes physical stricture of that segment of intestine. Gastric acid may reflux into the esophagus, leading to esophageal diseases including esophagitis, esophageal ulceration, and megaesophagus. Pseudo-obstruction (the loss of normal stomach outflow due to disrupted activity of the nervous system) of the gastric outflow may respond to aggressive therapy but ulceration that has led to fibrosis and stricture carries a guarded to poor prognosis. Clinical signs of gastric outflow obstruction include poor appetite, weight loss, spontaneous reflux, salivation, and intermittent and chronic colic that may worsen after eating. Diagnostic evaluation includes routine hematology and serum biochemistry and abdominal fluid evaluation. Endoscopic examination often provides direct visual evidence of a stricture or ulceration, allowing the veterinarian to decide on medical or surgical (particularly for strictures) treatment. If endoscopy is inconclusive, contrast radiography using barium or nuclear scintigraphy may be useful. On occasion, exploratory abdominal surgery is used to make a diagnosis.

Treatment of pseudo-obstruction may be instituted using a prokinetic drug to facilitate gastric emptying (see Chapter 4). Partial stricture of the pylorus may also respond to medical management of ulcers that may be present and to use of prokinetic medications. Severe strictures will require surgical bypass of the affected area of the pylorus or the duodenum. Persistent and/or progressive obstruction or pseudo-obstruction may lead to rupture of the stomach. The prognosis of this condition is guarded.

### Grain Overload

Anytime a horse ingests excessive amounts of carbohydrates it is at risk of developing problems associated with grain overload. A common scenario for such ingestion is the horse that gets into the feed room and eats large quantities of a grain or a feed concentrate. Soluble carbohydrate in the feed and its rapid ingestion becomes dangerous to the horse. However, horses fed large quantities of feed or horses that may not be used to ingesting such quantities are at risk of having problems associated with grain or carbohydrate overload. With this type of colic, soluble carbohydrates ingested exceed the amount that the small intestine can handle, and many of these carbohydrates then pass into the large intestine and the cecum. In these cases the carbohydrates are processed by many bacteria and produce a significant drop in the pH of the cecum and colon. This pH drop leads to the death of many bacteria in the large intestine and subsequent release of large quantities of endotoxin. The horse can then absorb the endotoxin. Excessive feeding or over-ingestion of corn and sweet feeds is associated with grain overload colic, but oats and other grains fed in excess or that are accidentally over-ingested may also lead to this situation.

Overeating can lead to colic.

Development of endotoxemia can occur after over-ingestion of soluble carbohydrates. Diarrhea, laminitis, and death may follow. Clinical signs of grain overload are not specific but include colic, distended abdomen, gastric reflux, laminitis, sweating, diarrhea, and trembling. Endotoxic and hypovolemic shock may lead to clinical signs associated with these conditions, including dark red mucous membranes, high heart rates, increased respiratory rate, and severe intestinal motility disturbances.

Seek immediate veterinary attention when any horse gains access and over-ingests grain or concentrated feeds. Veterinary attention may help minimize or prevent the development of clinical signs of colic, endotoxemia, and laminitis. Horses are usually managed by intubation with a nasogastric tube to check for gastric reflux and to administer medications. These medications may include activated charcoal, magnesium sulfate, or mineral oil to help prevent further absorption of endotoxins and to help coat and bind further carbohydrate-containing feedstuffs. Intravenous fluids may become necessary if and when a horse develops endotoxemia and dehydration due to grain overload and/or diarrhea. The volumes required may be high and electrolyte replacement may become necessary. Electrolyte and acid/base evaluation will be necessary to clarify which electrolytes are deficient or imbalanced. Plasma administration may become necessary with protein loss associated with diarrhea. Anti-endotoxic and anti-laminitic therapies are also often administered. This may include foot support and the administration of flunixin meglumine (Banamine®), acepromazine, aspirin, heparin, pentoxyfylline, and/or antihistamines. In severely dehydrated and shocky horses, hypertonic saline administration may be necessary, followed by high volumes of intravenous fluids.

### Blister Beetle Toxicosis (Cantharidin Toxicity)

Cantharidin is the toxin from blister beetles, or beetles of the *Epicauta* species. The beetles are termed blister beetles because of their production of blisters on the surfaces of many internal and external tissues. Blister beetle toxicosis occurs when a horse ingests infested alfalfa hay. Today's techniques of preparing alfalfa hay may include simultaneous cutting and crimping that entrap large numbers of these insects within the bales or flakes of the hay. Allowing time between cutting and baling permits the insects to leave the cut alfalfa hay.

The toxin produced by these beetles, cantharidin, is highly toxic to horses and ingestion of even a small number of insects may be fatal. The toxin persists in the beetle long after it dies. It causes rapid development of hypovolemic shock and significant pain due to the toxin activity on the surface of the mouth, gastrointestinal tract, and urinary tract. The clinical signs produced include heavy sweating, high heart rates, colic, frequent low-volume urination, red urine, red mucous membranes, dehydration, poor appetite, and submerging the muzzle in the water bucket. Electrolyte disturbances are common and can be severe. Severe hypocalcemia (low-blood calcium) may lead to muscle fasciculations (fine tremoring), stiff gait, and synchronous diaphragmatic flutter (thumps). Other disturbances may include low-blood magnesium and low levels of blood protein and kidney failure. Disease may be acute or have a prolonged onset over hours to days, depending on the number of beetles ingested.

A diagnosis is often made presumptively by history of alfalfa hay ingestion, presence of beetles in the hay, colic, low-blood calcium, frequent urination, red urine, and associated other clinical abnormalities. Definitive diagnosis is reached by isolation of the toxin from the urine or from the gastric contents. However, the toxin often becomes undetectable three to four days after toxin ingestion. Treatment is largely supportive and symptomatic. Activated charcoal or mineral oil is often administered by nasogastric tube to absorb cantharidin that may persist in the intestinal tract. Intravenous fluids are administered to treat dehydration and to promote increased urination and "flushing" of the kidney tubules of toxin and blood from the ulcerated areas of the lower urinary tract. Electrolytes are required and supplied in the intravenous fluids. These include calcium and magnesium supplementation. Intestinal protectants such as sucralfate are often administered to help treat the inflamed and ulcerated intestinal tract. Pain management is necessary. However, non-steroidal anti-inflammatory drugs may be ineffective for pain relief and may best be avoided due to their potential to produce and further perpetuate intestinal ulceration. Broad-spectrum antibiotics may be administered to prevent infection or sepsis due to the damage of the intestinal barrier. There is no specific antidote for cantharidin toxicosis. Prognosis for horses suffering from cantharidin toxicosis varies and depends on the amount of toxin ingested and severity of clinical signs. Severe cases carry a poor prognosis for survival.

### Cecal Rupture

Cecal rupture may occur without obvious indications of impending rupture. Its causes are often unknown. Cecal rupture may be seen in horses hospitalized for other medical problems. Administration of non-steroidal anti-inflammatory drugs may be an added risk for cecal rupture. These drugs may cause changes in cecal motility or mask clinical signs associated with cecal impaction. Mares that have recently foaled may be at higher risk of cecal rupture from trauma to the cecum induced during foaling and from changes in cecal motility that lead to impaction or gas distension of the cecum around the time of foaling. During foaling the increases in abdominal pressure may lead to cecal perforation of the impacted or gas-distended cecum. Clinical signs of cecal perforation are those associated with rupture of intestine. Signs of cecal impaction may occur prior to rupture and include mild colic, poor appetite, depression, and scant fecal production. Once rupture has occurred, clinical signs may include depression, colic, shaking, sweating, high heart rate, dehydration, and dark red mucous membranes. Rectal examination may reveal an enlarged and impacted cecum and a gritty feeling of fecal material on the outside surface of the intestine. As is the case with nearly any intestinal rupture, once cecal rupture has occurred the horse cannot be successfully treated and will require euthanasia.

### Rectal Tears

Rectal tears are a potential danger anytime a horse receives a rectal examination. However, certain factors make rectal tears more likely to occur during a rectal examination. Some of these factors may include dehydration, excessive straining during the examination, fractious behavior, inadequate restraint of the horse, and lack of adequate lubrication. A rectal tear occurs when there is a breach in the integrity of the rectal lining. The degree of tearing is graded from 1 to 4, depending on the depth of the tear. Tears are also described in terms of their location within the rectum. They often occur in the dorsal (top) half of the rectum at a distance of about 20 to 30 centimeters inside. Grade 1 tears are associated with a small amount of blood on the rectal sleeve and abrasion of the mucosa (lining) of the rectum. A grade 2 tear occurs with complete disruption of the mucosa into the muscular layer of the rectum. A grade 3 tear is present when the entire mucosa and muscular layer of the rectum are torn with only the outermost layer of tissue persisting (the serosa). A grade 4 tear is complete disruption of all intestinal layers such that a hole through the rectum opens into the abdomen of the horse.

All equine veterinarians are extremely cautious and concerned about the safety and execution of rectal examinations. Despite good technique and safety measures to reduce the risks for tears, they sometimes occur. If blood from inside the rectum is discovered on a rectal sleeve following the examination, a veterinarian will assess the situation and often examine the rectum with a bare hand to evaluate for a tear and grade it. Following this assessment the veterinarian will determine a plan for managing the injury. Grade 3 and grade 4 tears require referral of the horse to a medical and surgical hospital because grade 3 tears often and easily advance to grade 4. The abdomen becomes contaminated with fecal material leaking through the tear and the horse develops endotoxemia and shock. Horses being referred to a hospital often have an intravenous catheter placed for fluids during extended shipping, are begun on intravenous antibiotics, and receive pain medication and anti-inflammatory drugs. Further preparation often includes rectal packing to prevent passage of fecal material into the tear and an epidural anesthetic for the same purpose.

Not all rectal tears occur in a region that will communicate with the abdomen. Some tears occur closer to the anus. Although these tears may carry a better prognosis with appropriate attention, they must be immediately addressed to prevent fecal material from accumulating in the tear and therefore increasing the likelihood of the tear worsening to where it breaks open into the abdomen. The overall prognosis for rectal tears decreases with the grade of the tear such that grade 1 and 2 tears are most often managed successfully without referral and with a fair to good prognosis. Generally speaking, if surgical closure of grade 3 and 4 rectal tears can be made, the prognosis will be better than trying to manage the tear medically and allowing it to heal closed. Horses with grade 4 tears that cannot receive intensive care and management rapidly become candidates for euthanasia.

### Acute Pancreatitis

Pancreatitis is a rare cause of abdominal pain in the horse. The cause of this condition is usually unclear and a diagnosis before death is often not made since the clinical signs are very similar to that of other causes of severe acute colic (such as small intestinal strangulating conditions and anterior enteritis). Pancreatitis sometimes may be found in association with hyperlipemia (high blood fat). It has been proposed that fat may be deposited in and around the pancreas with hyperlipemia. The fat is subsequently broken down by a pancreatic fat enzyme, lipase, and then released as free fatty acids, which are toxic to the pancreas. Clinical signs of pancreatitis can include severe abdominal pain, shock, high heart rate, high respiratory rate, poor tissue perfusion, sweating, and distension of the stomach with copious amounts of nasogastric reflux. Specific diagnosis is made postmortem as abdominal fluid, rectal exam, and laboratory findings are often not specifically diagnostic. Affected horses die within 24 hours. Therapy for shock and abdominal pain may help temporarily.

## THINGS THAT MAY LOOK LIKE COLIC

### Esophageal Obstruction (Choke)

Esophageal obstruction or choke occurs anytime any feedstuff or other material becomes lodged in the horse's esophagus. Horses with esophageal obstruction do not exhibit true signs of colic (abdominal pain) because the intestines are not affected by this condition. However, horses may act strangely in ways that are interpreted by owners or caretakers as signs of colic. Horses may salivate excessively and/or have salivary discharge mixed with feed material coming from the nose. They may wretch and swallow excessively to try to pass the obstruction.

Choke is an emergency situation for several reasons. Any obstruction that persists in the esophagus for an extended period may lead to severe ulceration of the esophageal mucosa. Healing can lead to a stricture formation and/or abnormal motility of the esophagus such that recurrent esophageal obstruction becomes common. Horses with choke exhibit nasal discharge with feed material. This mixture is often aspirated into the trachea by the affected horse, possibly leading to severe pneumonia. Therefore, treatment of esophageal obstruction often includes antibiotics for a week or more beyond resolution of the obstruction. An externally palpable mass in the esophagus and/or inability to pass a nasogastric tube into the stomach also indicate choke.

Choke is usually initially managed on the farm. It involves the passage of a nasogastric tube into the esophagus and gentle lavage and manipulation of the obstruction using water and the nasogastric tube. Sedation is indicated because it helps lower the horse's head, reducing the risks of aspiration, and relaxes the esophageal musculature that often spasms around the obstruction. Most obstructions are relieved using this type of therapy.

Difficult cases of choke or cases that have been ongoing for longer than 24 hours should be considered for referral. Diagnostics at a referral hospital may include endoscopy and contrast radiography. Contrast radiography and endoscopy may be particularly important in helping identify predisposing factors for esophageal obstruction such as an esophageal stricture or esophageal diverticulum. These conditions may be present secondary to previous bouts of esophageal obstruction. As the duration of the obstruction increases, so, too, does the likelihood increase of complications involving the nerve supply of the esophagus and the esophagus itself. Severe cases are often placed on intravenous fluids because of reduced ability to drink water with the obstruction. Heavy sedation and trans-endoscopic manipulation of the obstruction are often attempted in the hospital environment.

Other medications may be administered to help relax the esophageal musculature such as oxytocin and repetitive doses of sedatives such as xylazine and detomodine. More aggressive therapy may become necessary with continued failure to resolve the obstruction. This may include general anesthesia to allow manipulation of the blockage trans-endoscopically or by nasogastric tube. Surgical approaches are uncommon and may increase the incidence of complications after healing.

### *Laminitis*

Laminitis is a disease that causes inflammation of the tissue that attaches the hoof wall to the bones inside the foot (known as the coffin bone or third phalanx or P3). Such inflammation is believed to be triggered by alterations in blood supply to the foot. The death of the attaching tissue, or laminae, can cause rotation and/or sinking of the coffin bone. Rotation or sinking of the coffin bone is also known as "founder."

Changes in blood supply to the foot are commonly associated with dehydration and/or endotoxemia. Therefore, horses that experience colic are probably at increased risk for developing laminitis. Certain types of colic such as diarrhea, anterior enteritis, grain overload, and any colic that requires surgical intervention are probably more likely to be associated with endotoxemia and pose greater risk for the development of laminitis.

Laminitis is an extremely painful condition. Many of the clinical signs of laminitis are similar to those exhibited by a horse with colic. Sweating, high heart rate, and rapid respiration are often present in acute and severe cases of laminitis. Horses with laminitis exhibit a characteristic stance or walk. Horses in severe pain exhibit a "camped out" stance with the forelimbs extended far out in front of the body and the hind limbs far underneath the body. This stance is adopted to help minimize the amount of weight borne on the toes of the forelimbs. When these horses are asked to walk, they either refuse to do so or walk only very gingerly and with extreme difficulty as though on eggshells. Most horses refuse to permit a forelimb to be lifted. Some horses with laminitis will spend extensive periods lying down. Less severely affected horses may be more willing to walk but still exhibit the characteristic type of walk when they are able to do so. Management of horses with laminitis should include treatment of any conditions that lead to endotoxemia and shock. Other therapies include non-steroidal anti-inflammatory drugs and pain medications, foot and frog support, and corrective shoeing once the acutely painful condition has subsided. Horses that exhibit endotoxemia and shock are often also treated with anti-endotoxemic medications and anti-laminitic therapies such as heparin, acepromazine, aspirin, pentoxifylline, J5 plasma, polymixin B, and others.

### Pleuritis

Pleuritis is inflammation of the chest cavity. The condition is most commonly associated with pneumonia that has extended from the lungs into the chest cavity, but it can be associated with trauma or other primary ailments that exist in the chest cavity. Pleuritis leads to pain in the chest cavity (pleurodynia) and the signs of pain in the chest cavity can appear to be very similar to pain in the abdomen, including high respiratory and heart rates. Other potential clinical signs may include shallow breathing with nostril flare, sweating, trembling, nasal discharge, and unwillingness to move or walk. Management of pleuritis requires treatment of the primary problem, pain medications, and often, antibiotic administration.

### Urinary Problems

Horses that posture to urinate or that have difficulty urinating, especially geldings and stallions, may appear to be exhibiting signs of colic when they stretch out. It is usually obvious that a horse is posturing to urinate, though some horses may posture frequently and for prolonged periods. This is particularly true for horses with lower urinary tract obstruction, inflammation, or infections. The persistent stretching to urinate may be confused with stretching due to abdominal pain. Usually careful observation and detection of abnormal urination such as frequent posturing and low volumes of urine will indicate the stretching is more likely to be associated with a urinary tract problem rather than with an intestinal or colic problem. A veterinarian should be consulted to make this determination. If a urinary tract problem is suspected, a complete evaluation of the urinary tract is warranted. This includes a rectal examination that permits concurrent evaluation of the intestinal tract and the lower urinary tract.

### Foaling

During stage 1 of labor, the mare becomes uncomfortable as the fetus repositions in preparation for delivery. The manifestation of this is indeed a form of colic, since it is abdominal pain. However, discomfort at this stage is expected and appropriate. It is associated with fetal repositioning in preparation for birth. It is probably prudent to check breeding dates and to ascertain whether foaling is expected to help to interpret the cause of the colic. Mares not due to foal may either be aborting the fetus or exhibiting colic due to intestinal tract problem(s) rather than fetal repositioning. If there is any question about the cause, consult with a veterinarian. Mares that exhibit pain associated with labor for extended periods may be having trouble delivering the foal (dystocia), a situation that requires immediate veterinary attention.

### Medications

A few commonly administered medications are associated with producing discomfort and abdominal pain. The most commonly encountered of such medications are probably prostaglandin F2a (Lutalyse) and oxytocin. Prostaglandin is used in mares to help time ovulation for breeding. This medication is administered to "short-cycle" and sometimes causes heavy sweating and mild to moderate colic. The effects generally last about one hour or so. Oxytocin is administered either to induce foaling or more commonly to help evacuate the uterus of fluid and debris after foaling. It causes uterine contraction in mares and consequently produces mild colic.

### Blood in the Abdomen (Hemoperitoneum)

Blood in the abdomen may be caused by a number of conditions, including rupture of a uterine artery in a broodmare as previously discussed. Other conditions leading to bleeding in the abdomen can include rupture of the spleen, liver, or kidney, a blood-clotting disorder, cancer in the abdomen, post-castration bleeding, and arterial lacerations due to trauma. The clinical signs most commonly seen with bleeding in the abdomen are those associated with shock due to hemorrhage and loss of blood volume. This may include heavy sweating, high heart rate, high respiratory rate, weak pulses, pale membranes, trembling, and weakness. Ultrasound of the abdomen with or without abdominal fluid evaluation generally confirms bleeding in the abdomen. Management involves treating the cause of the bleeding, careful management of shock, and prevention of further bleeding. This can involve intravenous fluids, blood transfusions, Oxyglobin, pain management, naloxone, aminocaproic acid, intranasal oxygen therapy, and perhaps surgical correction. Careful monitoring of blood pressure is required to prevent excessively high blood pressures with fluid or transfusion therapy that could lead to further bleeding.

## CHRONIC/RECURRENT COLIC

Chronic colic can be defined as persistent abdominal pain for longer than a few days' duration. Most horses that exhibit abdominal pain for extended periods exhibit intermittent and recurrent bouts of mild to moderate colic. Chronic and recurrent colic is less likely to be associated with complete obstruction and strangulating obstruction since these conditions lead to rapid and severe deterioration of the horse's stability and overall health.

Clinical signs of chronic/recurrent colic include either persistent (chronic) or intermittent mild to moderate abdominal pain (recurrent) (see Chapter 1). However, some horses may not overtly display mild abdominal pain. Other clinical signs that may indicate abdominal pain and intestinal problems include abnormally slow feed intake, poor appetite, depression, lethargy, failure to maintain body weight, poor hair coat, and weakness.

Chronic and recurrent colic are often initially managed by standard on-farm treatments. However, with persistent pain or recurring episodes of colic, further diagnostics are probably indicated to pinpoint the specific cause of the colic and facilitate appropriate therapy. Additional diagnostics are chosen by the examining veterinarian based on clinical signs exhibited by the horse and results of preliminary diagnostics. A number of diagnostics commonly employed for the evaluation of chronic and recurrent colic include complete blood count and serum biochemistry, abdominal fluid evaluation, rectal examination, abdominal ultrasonography, and evaluation of the stomach by endoscope (gastroscopy). The list of potential causes of chronic colic is extensive; however, some more of the more commonly encountered conditions are presented below.

Chronic/recurrent colic can be very difficult to diagnose. Consequently, it often becomes necessary to use other much less commonly employed diagnostic techniques. These diagnostics, described in Chapter 2, may include carbohydrate absorption tests, other specific blood parameter evaluations, rectal biopsy, fecal cultures, exploratory laparoscopy, exploratory abdominal surgery, intestinal or other abdominal biopsy, and others.

## MAJOR MEDICAL CONDITIONS ASSOCIATED WITH CHRONIC COLIC AND/OR WEIGHT LOSS

### Parasitism

Intestinal parasitism has been strongly associated with chronic and recurrent colic. The incidence of parasitism as a cause of chronic colic has probably been reduced substantially in the past 10 to 20 years with the creation of better deworming medications, improved owner education on parasite control, and better owner compliance in adopting these recommended deworming strategies. However, parasites will continue to be important to consider in the evaluation of chronic and recurrent colic. The danger of migrating strongyle larvae is always important for the owner and attending veterinarian to consider in designing an appropriate deworming program. Today's deworming programs are also designed to manage and control infestation with small stronglyes (cyathostomes). These parasites are commonly associated with recurrent colic due to their ability to encyst within the small intestine, where they may affect motility and physiologic function of the intestine.

Frequently, a reasonable approach to the treatment of chronic colic may involve the administration of a "larvicidal dose" of a benzimidazole dewormer to address possible small strongyle infestations. Fecal examination is often performed to identify small strongyle eggs in the feces; however, in the author's experience, clinical improvement may be seen with benzimidazole administration despite failure to identify small strongyle eggs in the feces. The appropriate dosing requires administration of much higher levels of the dewormer on a three- to five-day basis. The most commonly administered medication for this treatment is probably fenbendazole (Panacur®, Safe-Gard®). It may then be advisable to follow this dosing with ivermectin at four to six weeks followed by pyrantel (Strongid) another four to six weeks later (sequentially administered: fenbendazole, ivermectin, pyrantel each four to six weeks apart). Pyrantel may be substituted with new ivermectin formulations that also contain praziquintel.

### Ulcers

Intestinal ulcers can occur in the stomach, small intestine, and large colon. The clinical manifestations of intestinal ulceration have been addressed more completely earlier in this chapter. Ulcers may lead to anything from mild abdominal pain to general malaise, poor appetite, and weight loss. Horses may lose protein and blood in the stool.

Ulcers are commonly associated with chronic or recurrent colic. However, it is important to realize that intestinal ulceration may be present in many horses that do not experience chronic colic. Therefore, if and when a diagnosis of gastric or other ulceration is made, it should not preclude the consideration of other conditions that may cause chronic colic. Indeed, intestinal ulceration may be present *due* to the primary cause of colic without it being the *reason* for the chronic abdominal pain.

As in treating parasitism as a cause of colic, intestinal ulceration is often treated empirically without specific diagnosis of the condition or without certainty that ulceration has caused the chronic/recurrent colic. Response to treatment is evaluated. If the horse has failed to respond by cessation or significant reduction in the degree and frequency of abdominal pain, more aggressive diagnostics are likely to be necessary. Right dorsal colitis is highly associated with non-steroidal anti-inflammatory drug administration. Therapy for gastric and small intestinal ulcers primarily hinges on the administration of anti-ulcer medication, particularly omeprazole. Large intestinal ulceration is often conservatively managed by dietary changes and other potentially helpful treatments (see section on Large Intestinal Enteritis/right dorsal colitis).

### Impactions

Intestinal impactions may cause mild to moderate chronic colic. Impactions may cause incomplete obstruction of the intestine; thus, the abdominal pain may wax and wane in severity. Intestinal impactions that cause chronic colic are probably most commonly associated with large intestinal impactions, particularly pelvic flexure impactions. The diagnosis and management of intestinal impactions as the cause of colic have been outlined in the section earlier in this chapter.

### Gastrointestinal Infiltrative Diseases (Chronic Inflammatory Diseases)

Intestinal diseases that cause infiltration and inflammation of the intestine may disrupt the normal physiological mechanisms that work in the intestinal tract. This can include normal motility and absorptive function. These conditions may lead to chronic colic and weight loss. With infiltrative disease of the small intestine, it is not uncommon to see reduced nutrient absorptive capacity. A carbohydrate absorption test can identify malabsorption. Intestinal loss of protein may occur alone or concurrently with malabsorption.

Chronic inflammatory intestinal disease is a catchall term that refers to a number of intestinal infiltrative diseases. This group of diseases may affect the small and large intestine, lymph nodes, and other organs in the abdomen. The infiltrate of the intestine is usually composed of inflammatory cells that may be of one predominant type or may be mixed in population. Cell type(s) determine the type of infiltrative disease. Examples of such diseases include eosinophilic enteritis, granulomatous enteritis, and lymphocytic-plasmacytic enteritis. Granulomatous enteritis tends to be more common in horses between one and five years of age and over-represented in Standardbreds. Certain types of infection of the intestinal tract may lead to granulomatous enteritis. Bacteria such as *Mycobacterium tuberculosis* or some fungal organisms may produce granulomatous enteritis. Eosinophilic enteritis involves the infiltration of eosinophils and lymphocytes in the small intestine. The cause of this condition is also unclear but could be related to parasitism or a more diffusely occurring disease that causes infiltration of many different organs with eosinophils (a specific type of inflammatory cell). Affected organs may include the skin, liver, and pancreas. Lymphocytic-plasmacytic enteritis is characterized by infiltration of the intestine by lymphocytes and plasma cells without evidence of granulomatous inflammation (similar cell types involved without evidence of granuloma formation as seen with granulomatous enteritis).

Lymphosarcoma is a cancerous condition that can lead to multiple organ involvement, including the intestinal tract. The condition may lead to focal tumor development in the intestinal tract or to diffuse infiltration of segments of intestine by tumor cells. Diffuse infiltration with tumor cells then often leads to inhibited absorption in both the small and the large intestine. Ulceration of the affected intestine may occur in association with lymphosarcoma of the intestinal tract. This can lead to significant protein and blood loss in addition to impaired absorption. Frequently, abdominal lymph nodes are also affected and may become enlarged and are another potential source for development of colic.

Clinical signs of infiltrative intestinal diseases include diarrhea, chronic/recurrent colic, poor appetite, weight loss, depression and lethargy, development of edema, fever, and skin lesions. A diagnosis of any of these diseases may be difficult to reach. Complete blood count and serum biochemical analysis often produce non-specific findings. Rectal examination may be helpful if abnormally thickened intestine or lymph node enlargement is palpated. Ultrasound examination may reveal thickened intestinal walls. Carbohydrate absorption tests often are useful in identifying intestinal malabsorption. However, specific diagnosis will likely require biopsy of an affected segment of intestine. Culture may be required to identify specific bacterial involvement. Rectal biopsy may be attempted in the standing horse. However, horses with these conditions may not exhibit microscopic changes representative of the condition in the rectum. Biopsy of other segments of intestine may require laparoscopic surgery or routine exploratory abdominal surgery.

The overall prognosis of any of these conditions is guarded to very poor. Usually, by the time the condition is recognized and diagnosed, the progression of the disease is highly advanced. Horses with diffuse lymphosarcoma cannot be humanely managed and should be euthanized. Palliative therapy for other infiltrative intestinal diseases may include feeding highly digestible diets and high-quality fiber. Increasing feed intake is probably best performed by increasing the frequency rather than the amounts at the same intervals. Frequently, steroidal (corticosteroid) therapy is used to help control the amount of inflammation and infiltration of the intestine. This therapy is usually of limited benefit. Some cases of lymphocytic-plasmacytic enteritis may benefit transiently from administration of dexamethasone (a corticosteroid). Surgical resection of affected areas may help, but the condition most often affects too much intestine to warrant resection.

### Abdominal Abscesses

Abscess formation in the abdomen often occurs in association with the mesentery or the abdominal organs as a complication from strangles (*Streptococcus equi* subspecies *equi*). Abscess formation may also be associated with a site of intestinal leakage from a foreign body perforation of the intestine, perforation of an ulcer, abdominal trauma, leakage/contamination from a surgical site, or following castration. Occasionally, the cause of an abscess may be unclear. Other bacteria that have been associated with abdominal abscesses include *Streptococcus equi* subspecies *zooepidemicus*, *Escherichia coli*, *Salmonella* species, *Rhodococcus equi*, and various types of anaerobic bacteria.

Clinical signs of abdominal abscessation may include chronic weight loss; acute, chronic, or recurrent colic; fever; poor appetite; depression; and diarrhea. A diagnosis of an abdominal abscess can be difficult to reach. Typically, diagnostics may include hematology and serum biochemistry, rectal examination, abdominal fluid evaluation, ultrasonography, nuclear scintigraphy, laparoscopy, and routine exploratory abdominal surgery.

Treatment involves appropriate antibiotic administration based on culture and sensitivity (if possible). Some abscesses may resolve with antibiotic therapy alone. Antibiotic therapy is often necessary for prolonged periods, in many cases up to six months or longer. Treatment is usually continued until clinical signs and laboratory parameters have returned to normal. Surgical intervention and drainage of an abscess are often considered but seldom possible due to the location and potential for contamination of the abdomen with peritonitis. The overall prognosis for treatment of abdominal abscesses, without complication, is usually guarded to good. Prognosis becomes poorer if and when abdominal adhesions form.

### Intestinal Neoplasia

Intestinal neoplasia (cancer) is uncommon in horses.

Tumors have been reported in nearly all segments and tissues of the intestinal tract, but certain locations and types of tissue are more commonly affected. Clinical signs of intestinal neoplasia are not specific for neoplasia. They can include poor appetite, weight loss, poor digestion, poor absorption, protein and/or blood loss from the intestinal tract, depression, lethargy, and other associated organ dysfunction. From this list it is easy to see that none of the signs are specific for intestinal neoplasia. They are shared with a large number of other diseases and conditions that may affect the intestinal tract and other organ systems. Furthermore, the incidence of intestinal neoplasia is low, estimated to be less than 0.1% of all postmortem examinations and only about 5% of horses with clinical signs of abdominal diseases. Therefore, it is important to remember to evaluate horses with these clinical signs completely, in order to identify more commonly occurring conditions before focusing on intestinal neoplasia as a diagnosis. Diagnostic testing that may be performed to evaluate horses with these non-specific clinical signs often include hematology and serum biochemistry, ancillary blood parameter evaluations, rectal examination, abdominal fluid evaluation, ultrasonography, carbohydrate absorption testing, nuclear scintigraphy, laparoscopy, and occasionally routine exploratory celiotomy. These diagnostic tests are used for evaluation of abdominal diseases and are not neoplasia-specific. Surgical biopsy of an affected area will help to identify any neoplastic mass found by these diagnostic techniques.

Primary tumors affecting the intestinal tract of the horse are uncommon. However, when a neoplastic (cancerous) mass or tissue is found, it is most likely to be one of the following types:

• lipoma that affects the mesentery of the small or large intestine,

• squamous cell carcinoma that affects the stomach and esophagus,

• lymphosarcoma that affects small and large intestine,

• adenocarcinoma that affects the small and large intestine,

• leiomyoma that affects the small intestine and small colon,

• leiomyosarcoma that affects the stomach, small intestine, and rectum, and

• myxosarcoma that affects the cecum.

Treatment of primary tumors of the intestinal tract is generally unrewarding. Systemic corticosteroids help temporarily, and anabolic steroids may be necessary to help maintain weight. A few anti-cancer drugs have been used on a limited basis and have shown some short-term benefits in horses with intestinal neoplasia. Such agents tend to be rather expensive and not always successful. Ultimately the prognosis for horses with intestinal neoplasia is poor.

### Peritonitis

Numerous conditions can cause peritonitis in the horse. Peritonitis is an inflammation of the abdominal cavity and may be associated with intestinal leakage or contamination from a surgical site in the abdomen, abdominal abscess, leaking ulcers of the intestine, trauma, primary infection due to spreading from another organ or by the blood, and other causes. Diagnosis of peritonitis is made by hematology and serum biochemical evaluation, abdominal fluid evaluation and culture, and ultrasound examination. Other diagnostics are often necessary to help rule out other conditions and/or to identify the cause of the peritonitis.

Some clinicians consider septic peritonitis to be a surgical condition. Surgery is performed to evaluate the abdomen for a cause of the peritonitis, to facilitate correction of the underlying cause, and to perform a complete abdominal lavage. Treatment includes antibiotic administration for septic peritonitis. On occasion abdominal lavage is performed without exploratory surgical intervention by placement of a large-bore rubber or other type of catheter into the abdomen through a stab incision. The catheter is then used to instill large volumes of fluid into the abdomen. The fluid, which sometimes contains antibiotics, is permitted to remain in the abdomen for some time and is subsequently drained through the same rubber catheter. Potassium penicillin in addition to an aminoglycoside such as gentamicin and oral metronidazole are often used for systemic antibiotic therapy. Pain management and anti-inflammatory medications are also employed in addition to antibiotic therapy. More severe cases may require treatment for shock and endotoxemia. Overall prognosis depends on the cause, duration, and severity of the peritonitis. Response to therapy can help provide overall prognosis on a case-by-case basis.

### Right Dorsal Colitis

Right dorsal colitis might be associated with chronic colic and weight loss in the horse. This condition is often associated with the administration of non-steroidal anti-inflammatory drugs. A more complete definition of this condition has been addressed under the sections on Intestinal Ulceration and Intestinal Enteritis.

### Liver and Biliary Disease

Liver disease is relatively uncommon in horses. It can be associated with clinical signs of weight loss and poor appetite, jaundice, central nervous system disorders, and colic. Liver disease may be acute or chronic in nature. Acute liver failure can be associated with administration of biologics of equine origin such as tetanus antitoxin. This condition is referred to as Theiler's disease. Acute liver failure may also occur from toxin ingestion. Acute liver failure can present with severe jaundice, nervous dysfunction (such as profound depression and head pressing), and blood clotting abnormalities. Chronic liver disease may be associated with pyrrolizidine alkaloid intoxication from various types of poisonous plants. Poor pasture and overgrazing probably increase the likelihood that horses would ingest plants to which they would normally show aversion. Biliary disease may also occur from ascending bacterial infections from the small intestine. In some cases horses may develop biliary obstruction from "sludging" in the bile canals due to "stones" in the same canals. Diagnosis of liver disease is made by hematology and serum biochemical analysis with elevations in liver-specific enzymes, liver function tests (such as serum bile acid evaluation), ultrasound examination of the liver, and liver biopsy.

Management of liver disease depends on the etiology. Treatment of severe acute liver disease is primarily supportive in nature. Horses that survive for five days without worsening may recover. When neurological signs (including seizures) associated with hepatitic encephalopathy due to acute liver failure cannot be controlled, prognosis for recovery is probably poor. Chronic liver disease and biliary tract disease may respond to antibiotics and supportive care including good nutrition that minimizes overproduction of ammonia from high levels of protein in the diet. Biliary obstructions (stones) detected by ultrasound or other diagnostic imaging techniques can be removed surgically. Other conditions that affect the liver may include liver abscesses, hyperlipemia and fatty liver, neoplasia, and other masses. Their management is often similar to that for other liver diseases.

## NERVOUS SYSTEM-RELATED CAUSES OF COLIC

Conditions that affect the nervous system of the horse have the potential to cause colic. However, they are probably more commonly associated with weight loss. Horses affected with nervous system diseases that exhibit colic and/or weight loss will often also exhibit overt clinical signs of nervous system impairment. Therefore, the physical examination of such horses often involves a complete nervous system examination. The diagnostics performed on these horses are interpreted in the context of nervous system dysfunction with weight loss and/or colic occurring together as manifestations of a single disease process.

### Equine Dysautonomia (Grass Sickness)

This disease is the result of damage to the nerves of the autonomic (involuntary) nervous system, the enteric nervous system (nerves of the intestinal tract), and the somatic (voluntary) nervous system. This disease is not found in the United States but appears to be prevalent in Scotland, England, and countries of northern Europe. The specific cause of grass sickness is unknown. It affects horses between the ages of two and seven. Clinical signs of the disease depend on the form (acute, subacute, chronic). Signs may vary from depression, colic, high heart rate, muscle tremors, salivation, and gastric reflux in the acute form to severe weight loss, muscle tremors, mild colic, dysphagia (abnormal swallowing), and slightly elevated heart rate in the chronic form. Microscopic examination of lesions in the autonomic and enteric nerve ganglia postmortem diagnose the condition. Antemortem diagnosis may be achieved by surgical biopsy of the affected intestine. In many cases a presumptive diagnosis is made by the history and clinical signs. Acute cases may be difficult to distinguish from surgical colic. Treatment of grass sickness is often frustrating and unrewarding. Chronic cases may offer the best opportunity for management, which focuses on nursing and supportive care. Nutritional support is important and on occasion, prokinetic drugs may help support intestinal motility and reduce colic. Pain management is often necessary using non-steroidal anti-inflammatory drugs. Appetite stimulants are also often necessary. Horses that survive may be capable of returning to work. However, the prognosis for acute and subacute forms of this disease is not good.

### Equine Motor Neuron Disease

Equine motor neuron disease is a degenerative disease that affects the central nervous system. This equine disease has a human counterpart known as amyotrophic lateral sclerosis (ALS) or Lou Gehrig's disease. Affected horses may easily be confused with horses exhibiting chronic colic because the disease causes significant weight loss despite a good appetite, and affected horses tend to spend large amounts of time in recumbency. While standing, many horses exhibit a very narrow stance with all four legs placed closely to one another beneath the abdomen. Other clinical signs include muscle trembling and frequent weight shifting. Many breeds appear to be affected, but Quarter Horses are over-represented. Obvious signs of an uncoordinated gait are not usually present. A definitive cause of EMND is unknown. Low levels of vitamin E and superoxide dismutase are consistently associated with the disease but are probably not the sole causes. A significant association has also been identified between EMND and increased levels of copper in the CNS tissues and increased levels of iron in the liver. Lack of pasture appears to be a risk factor in the development of EMND.

An antemortem diagnosis is supported by clinical signs, retinal and/or dental pigmentation, and elevation in serum muscle enzyme levels. Biopsy of the sacrodorsalis medialis coccygeal muscle may provide microscopic evidence supportive of the disease. Biopsy of the spinal accessory nerve microscopically evaluated by an experienced neuropathologist can provide a definitive diagnosis.

Treatment is based on symptomatic and supportive care in addition to minimizing occurrence of factors associated with the disease. Horses with little or no pasture and/or hay should be tested for vitamin E levels and supplemented as needed.

### Other Nervous System Diseases

Muscle atrophy and weight loss can also occur as a result of neurological diseases in the horse. When the disease affects the central nervous system, other clinical signs of nervous system impairment usually occur. These signs are most often identified with cranial nerve and gait analysis of the affected horse. Conditions that cause central nervous system disease are not commonly associated with overt colic in the horse, but muscle atrophy and weight loss may become apparent over time, making these horses appear similar to horses that suffer from chronic disease affecting the intestinal system or abdominal organs. These diseases include equine protozoal myeloencephalitis and other less common nervous system diseases.

## MINIMIZING THE LIKELIHOOD OF COLIC

Practices that minimize colic in horses will also maximize the maintenance of their body condition. The beginning of this book included a discussion pertaining to anatomy and the physiology of digestion as important aspects of equine intestinal function and nutrition. The old adage that pastured horses seldom colic is probably not an exaggeration. Continual grazing appears to be significantly associated with reduced incidence of colic. In today's world horses do not always have unlimited access to pasture. Furthermore, owner convenience and land restriction have taken precedence over more natural feeding practices. Therefore, today most owners and caretakers feed concentrates in the form of grains, sweet feeds, and pelleted feeds. Feed companies today have been very helpful in developing appropriate concentrated feeds. However, as discussed in the Introduction, it is always possible to overfeed these concentrates, and as a general rule no more than five pounds of any concentrate should be fed at any feeding.

A good feeding practice that helps reduce the incidence of colic probably begins with a feeding program designed for the individual horse. This requires a thorough evaluation of the horse's use and age. Activity level, stage of growth, and, for broodmares, stage of gestation or lactation are all significant considerations for energy and nutrient requirements. The feeding program should be based on the forage, not the concentrate fed in the diet. Some horses that do not engage in heavy activity are probably best fed on forage only, including pasture grasses and/or supplemental hay. Concentrates should only be fed to meet the energy requirements that extend beyond what the forage in the diet meets. This depends on the amount of access to forages, the intestinal fill limit, and the quality of the forage. For feeding concentrate it is best and "more natural" for the horse to receive smaller amounts more often than offering large quantities once or twice a day. The appropriate development of a feeding program has been covered in other texts in Eclipse Press' *The Horse* Health Care Library. Consult these books and/or other reliable sources to maximize feeding efficiency and reduce the incidence of colic.

The quality of feed and forage may affect the incidence of colic. In general, it is probably better to feed high-quality forages from square bales rather than from round bales. Remember, younger cured forages will have higher levels of digestible fiber, and over-mature forage will have higher levels of non-digestible fiber (lignin). Furthermore, round bales are associated with high amounts of molds and decaying plant material. These characteristics of round bales can cause reactive and recurrent airway disease and exposure to botulism spores. Digestibility is an important consideration in palatable feed concentrates. As a horse ages, it may become less and less efficient at digesting and extracting nutrients from grains and concentrated feeds. Certain feed formulations offer older horses and horses with intestinal inefficiency more easily digestible feeds. Changing from one feed or hay type to another is best done gradually. Mixing of the two types of feed by increasing the relative amount of the "new" feed can be done over several days. This practice probably helps the horse adapt to the new feed type without developing acute intestinal problems or colic because of an abrupt change. Feeding horses at about the same time of day may also help minimize intestinal upset; however, this does not require minute-by-minute accounting of feed practices. Some horses eat their concentrates or grains very aggressively. This rapid ingestion of feed concentrate ("bolting") may also be associated with intestinal upsets and choke. Placing a salt block in the feed bucket may help to reduce bolting of feed and rapid consumption of large quantities of high concentrate grains and feeds. Horses that cannot tolerate unlimited access to lush pastures may be muzzled to prevent over-ingestion of such grass. This may be preferable to keeping the horse in a dry lot or locked in a stall for extended periods. Various types of muzzles can be used. Some will permit minimal grazing through the muzzle, while other muzzles will prevent grazing completely. Appropriately designed muzzles will permit uninhibited drinking to occur.

Of course, other routine care will help minimize colic in the horse. These practices include a good deworming program against all major parasites and one that minimizes cyathostome (small strongyles) parasites. In addition to adequate parasite control (which includes overall farm management in addition to deworming individual horses), regular dental care may also help reduce the incidence of colic on the farm. Such practice helps to prevent inadequate mastication of feed, quidding, and painful conditions associated with the mouth that may lead to weight loss and colic.

A regular physical examination for your horse is just as important as it is for people. This regular examination allows your veterinarian to become well acquainted with your horse's specific needs and conditions, permits early identification of potentially important conditions, and allows you to establish a good relationship with your veterinarian for routine and emergency care. This relationship is maximized when you and your veterinarian have an agreement and understanding of how you wish your horse to be handled in a colic situation that may require referral. It also permits the veterinarian to be comfortable with making decisions on your behalf should you or a primary caretaker be unavailable. Routine health care by your regular veterinarian includes vaccinations, regular physical examinations, necessary blood evaluations, and consultation on nutrition and management. Keeping your horse in good general health will help reduce the incidence of colic. Your veterinarian is an excellent resource for this, so establish a relationship with him or her and use this resource.

# CHAPTER 4

## Veterinary Management of Colic

Once a veterinarian has assessed a horse that is exhibiting colic, he/she will determine how to manage the colic. In some instances a horse might require immediate pain relief before the examination can begin.

### PAIN MANAGEMENT

#### Non-Steroidal Anti-Inflammatory Drugs (NSAIDs)

Non-steroidal anti-inflammatory drugs are anti-inflammatory medications with pain-killing properties. They are the most commonly used class of pain medications for horses with abdominal pain. These medications include flunixin meglumine (Banamine®), phenylbutazone (Bute), ketoprofen (Ketofen®), and others less commonly used for pain management (Ramifenazone, Eltenac). NSAIDs used to manage colic are most often given intravenously. However, flunixin meglumine and ketoprofen may also be administered in the muscle. Phenylbutazone cannot be given by any route other than intravenously because it leads to severe skin and tissue necrosis and sloughing. Of the NSAIDs, flunixin meglumine is most often administered for colic pain based on the belief that it has superior analgesic effects for pain emanating from the viscera (the organs). The duration of the pain-killing effects of these medications depends highly on the underlying cause and severity of the colic. Masking of colic that requires surgery has often been a concern of using these medications; however, it is unlikely that this happens very commonly. The need for repetitive pain medications of any type may indicate that a colic requires surgery.

NSAIDs can reduce fevers for up to 24 hours or more. For this reason the owner and/or the veterinarian should evaluate rectal temperature with this in mind. NSAIDs may be toxic if administered too frequently, at doses that are too high, or for extended durations. Toxic side effects may include kidney damage and ulceration of the intestinal tract. Always tell the examining veterinarian about the use of any pain medication. Many of the NSAIDs, particularly flunixin meglumine and ketoprofen, have been suggested to exhibit effects that combat endotoxemia. Their use for this specific property may not require doses as high as those necessary for pain management, and, therefore, are likely to be less toxic when specifically used to combat endotoxemia.

> ## AT A GLANCE
>
> - NSAIDs are the most common pain medication for horses with abdominal pain.
>
> - Dehydration is common in horses that colic, and intravenous fluid therapy can help horses rehydrate.
>
> - Colic surgery is both diagnostic and therapeutic.

### Alpha-Adrenergic Sedative/Pain-killing Drugs

Other commonly used pain medications include the alpha-adrenergic agonist sedatives. In addition to their primary action in providing sedation, this particular class of drugs also provides significant pain relief through their activity in the nervous system. These medications include xylazine (Rompun®), detomidine (Dormosedan®), and, less commonly, romifidine. They are given either intravenously or intramuscularly. These medications are much more rapid and intensive painkillers but also have other effects that may reduce intestinal motility, heart rate, and blood pressure. These medications should be used only by a veterinarian or with strict veterinary oversight. Although handling of these compounds is relatively safe, accidental injection of a human with less than 1/2 cc of the less potent drug xylazine can lead to acute respiratory and cardiac arrest. Although these compounds are used primarily as sedatives, they exhibit significant analgesic effects. Repetitive use of these medications strongly suggests a need for surgical intervention. Depending on the severity of the underlying problem, pain-killing effects may be minimal to lasting 15 to 60 minutes. Xylazine usually has profound effects for 15 to 30 minutes. Detomidine can work for 30 to 60 minutes. Mild colic pain may be controlled for much longer duration using detomidine. Xylazine has been used alone or in combination with lidocaine for epidural anesthesia to manage pain or straining associated with the rectum (as in the case of rectal tears). Butorphanol is often used in combination with xylazine and detomidine for added pain-killing effects. Butorphanol appears to augment the pain-killing effects of the alpha-adrenergic agonists (xylaxine, detomidine). Veterinarians gauge response to pain medications as a major factor in deciding whether to refer a horse with colic.

### Other Sedatives

Acepromazine is another sedative commonly administered for colic episodes. Despite its common use this medication has little to no use in any colic case because it provides no analgesic effects. Acepromazine is contraindicated in many instances. Because acepromazine has no pain-killing properties but does provide sedation, the outward manifestations of pain may seem to improve with sedation though the horse has experienced no real pain relief. Furthermore, acepromazine causes significant dilation of blood vessels. This effect can be extremely dangerous in any debilitated, endotoxemic, and/or dehydrated animal that is already experiencing poor circulation. Administering acepromazine blocks the ability of these horses to constrict their vessels and maintain blood pressure, cardiac return, cardiac output, and organ perfusion. Due to the loss of these abilities, the result can be acute collapse of the colicky horse. Because most horses experiencing a colic episode are at substantial risk of dehydration, endotoxemia, and debilitation, acepromazine is contraindicated. Furthermore, numerous other medications are not only safer to give but more effective for pain.

### Opioid Pain-Killing Medications

Opioid pain-killing medications have been used extensively to help manage colic. Opioid medications are closely controlled schedule drugs that can only be administered by licensed individuals. The most commonly administered opioid drug is butorphanol (Torbugesic®). This medication is probably most often used in association with one of the two alpha-adrenergic agonists listed above. It may also be administered in association with a NSAID analgesic drug to help reduce the dose and thus the possible toxic effects of the NSAIDs. Butorphanol can be administered intramuscularly for prolonged effect. For persistent pain that has been determined *not* to require surgical intervention or for post-surgical pain, butorphanol can be administered as a continuous infusion to manage colic or other types of pain. Long-term use of butorphanol is restricted by its potential to decrease intestinal motility and by eventual loss of pain-killing abilities. Butorphanol is thought to provide intense pain relief, including severe abdominal pain. Side effects are relatively uncommon but can include central nervous system excitement and ataxia, particularly with high doses.

Morphine is another opioid medication. Although morphine is a potent analgesic, its side effects tend to be more commonly seen than those of butorphanol. Morphine is commonly associated with excitement and has profound effects on the reduction of progressive intestinal motility. Morphine can also be used as a continuous infusion or as a medication for epidural injection to provide analgesia of the very tail end of the horse, and to help prevent straining in cases of rectal tears.

Pethidine and pentazocine are not used often. Pethidine is associated with few side effects but also provides only slight to moderate analgesia for short duration. Pentazocine offers no significant advantages since its analgesic properties are less intense than those of even xylazine.

### Lidocaine for Persistent Pain Control

Continuous infusion of lidocaine successfully manages non-surgical abdominal pain. An appropriate amount of the drug is commonly added to a one-liter bag of fluid and delivered at a calculated rate to ensure continuous delivery to the patient. Depending on the concentration and rate, the one-liter bag is usually enough to provide medication for several hours. Lidocaine also can be used in colic cases to help stimulate intestinal motility. With persistent use lidocaine loses its pain-killing effects over several days. Clearly there are several applications of this drug in the management and treatment of colic. Lidocaine can be used alone or as part of a combination with xylazine for epidural anesthesia to prevent straining and pain associated with the rectum (for managing rectal tears).

### Spasmolytic Agents

Spasmolytic agents (agents that reduce intestinal contractions) have been used in the past to manage certain types of colic. However, the inability to easily and accurately differentiate spasmodic colic (intestinal spasm) from other causes of colic limits the use of these agents. Spasmolytic agents include atropine, hyoscine, and dipyrone. Atropine should not be administered to a horse with colic because its effects can be extremely long lasting (up to several days), producing generalized immobility of the intestinal tract (ileus). Hyoscine, which helps relax the intestinal wall, has shorter-lasting effects. However, it is unavailable in this country. Furthermore, its use presupposes the ability to distinguish spasmodic colic from other types of colic.

Dipyrone is no longer commercially available in the United States. However, numerous compounding pharmacies are now making their own formulations for veterinarians. Dipyrone has been suggested to exhibit analgesic effects in addition to its proposed spasmolytic effects. Its analgesic properties, if any, are probably extremely limited. Its spasmolytic effects are also probably mild at best. It is unclear how such a medication fits into a useful approach to medical management of horses exhibiting colic.

### Medications Delivered by Nasogastric Tube

Laxatives and other compounds are most often administered by nasogastric tube, the most common being mineral oil. Mineral oil is not a specific treatment and does not exhibit any effects that cure any specific cause of colic. It is often administered to horses exhibiting colic because it might help lubricate impacted ingesta and induce distension of the stomach, which then produces reflex motility in the rest of the intestinal tract. Mineral oil also might help bind and prevent endotoxin and/or other toxin absorption into the circulation. A 1,000-pound horse will receive one-half to one gallon of mineral oil through a nasogastric tube. It can be given once to several times a day. Smaller horses receive a smaller volume as their stomachs are also proportionally smaller. Mineral oil is probably most appropriate for horses that have either impaction colic or colic due to unknown cause as long as the nasogastric tube does not reveal gastric reflux. Horses should probably be checked for reflux prior to the administration of mineral oil. Mineral oil can be seen being passed with the feces in 12 hours. Retention of mineral oil beyond 24 hours may support the presumption of poor intestinal motility or obstruction. However, the significance of this finding must be interpreted on a case-by-case basis. If a horse initially receives mineral oil during a colic examination and subsequently requires another colic examination, passage of the nasogastric tube into the stomach may yield mineral oil that has not effectively passed down the intestinal tract. In such instances the veterinarian might decide to discontinue administration of mineral oil.

Magnesium sulfate (Epsom salts) can be administered by nasogastric tube if an impaction has been diagnosed. Magnesium sulfate acts as an osmotic agent, drawing water into the intestine. This mechanism serves to soften and help loosen the impacted fecal material. This treatment is commonly used to help treat pelvic flexure impactions (probably the most common type of recognized impaction). Horses that receive magnesium sulfate by nasogastric tube should be closely monitored for dehydration. The loss of body water into the intestine can dehydrate the horse if fluid requirements do not meet the losses triggered by the Epsom salts. This can be minimized simply by tubing alternately with water and magnesium sulfate. Magnesium sulfate administration usually does not exceed two to three times per day. Horses that do not receive water by nasogastric tube to maintain hydration should probably receive intravenous fluid therapy.

Other therapeutic agents delivered by nasogastric tube may include psyllium hydrophilic muciloid (Metamucil®), dioctyl sodium sulfosuccinate (DSS), and others. Metamucil® is often administered as a bulk laxative but is most commonly used to manage/treat sand colic. Despite this use, it is unclear how effective psyllium really is at removing sand from the equine intestinal tract. Many studies have indicated little effect on sand removal; however, clinical use of this compound is common for this condition. This may partially stem from the fact that there is really no other specific medical therapy for intestinal sand removal. Mineral oil has been used for this purpose, but it is not known whether it works effectively for sand removal. Daily administration of psyllium in the feed has also been suggested to help prevent and remove sand from the large intestine.

DSS is used occasionally to treat impaction colic, mainly of the large intestine. DSS is associated with "breakdown" of the impaction (usually intestinal ingesta), primarily on the surface of the impaction. This may help loosen the impaction so it can pass down the intestinal tract for elimination. However, DSS can be highly irritating to the intestinal surface and cause inflammation of the intestinal mucosa in many sites along the tract. Furthermore, presumably due to this effect, one report linked the use of DSS in colic and the development of hypocalcemia (low blood calcium).

Water is also often administered by nasogastric tube to help maintain hydration and soften impactions. This is particularly useful when the administration of intravenous fluids is either impractical or financially impossible. When water is delivered to hydrate a horse and to help soften an impaction, it is probably necessary to administer it by nasogastric tube several times a day. Water alone or water with electrolytes can be administered. Occasionally, a nasogastric tube is left in the horse. This permits a "pop-off" valve if and when reflux accumulates in the stomach. An experienced caretaker can periodically draw off the reflux. Because it is important to confirm that the nasogastric tube remains in the stomach, this is not a practical option without a skilled caretaker(s).

### Trocharization

Horses with severe gas distension may be candidates for trocharization. This procedure relieves gas from the large intestine. It also can temporarily reduce abdominal pain associated with the distended large intestine. This procedure is not performed for small intestinal gas release. Most often, a large-bore intravenous catheter is used on the right flank. The area is prepared by sterile cleansing, and the catheter is introduced through the body wall into the large intestine. Usually, the site on the right side is used in order to trocharize the cecum of the horse. The cecum is normally the location of choice for trocharization due to its predictable location against the body wall and its tendency to become distended with large intestinal upset. However, trocharization of other segments of large intestine may also be performed safely as long as the intestine is close to the body wall of the horse. Large intestinal distension near a body wall is detected by a combination of rectal examination, listening for a "ping" sound with abdominal auscultation and percussion, and by ultrasound guidance (if necessary). A ping is detected with the stethoscope and a finger-flicking motion of the horse's flank. The sound that helps indicate gas-distended intestine sounds like a playground ball that hits the pavement and produces a "ping" sound. Occasionally, relief of gas distension may be all that is required to allow the intestine to resume normal function and/or position. However, more often this procedure provides only transient pain relief (if at all). Persistent pain and repeated need for trocharization may indicate the possible need for surgical intervention. Horses that are trocharized may be treated with antibiotics to help prevent peritonitis. Horses that are not surgical candidates may require repeat trocharization and heavy pain medication. In horses that are not surgical candidates, intractable pain that cannot be managed with pain medication and trocharization is an indication for euthanasia.

## INTRAVENOUS FLUID THERAPY AND CARDIOVASCULAR SUPPORT

Intravenous fluid therapy for colic usually has many benefits and is seldom contraindicated. However, the cost and administration of intravenous fluids can add significant expense to managing the horse with colic. Therefore, when a horse is not dehydrated or is only slightly dehydrated, stable, and not exhibiting reflux from the nasogastric tube, oral fluid therapy administered by a nasogastric tube rather than intravenously will minimize expense. However, expenses will add up in "call fees" to have the veterinarian back to administer the fluid by the nasogastric tube.

The major indications and benefits of intravenous fluid therapy in colic cases include 1) correcting dehydration, 2) stabilizing blood flow and tissue and organ blood perfusion, 3) improving intestinal motility, 4) providing fluid that can be transferred to the intestine to help soften impactions, and 5) correcting electrolyte and acid base imbalances. Dehydration is fairly common in horses that exhibit colic. In more severe colic situations and in horses that have diarrhea, dehydration can be very severe and lead to shock. When dehydration is moderate to severe, it is usually impractical and often impossible to correct fluid deficits simply by administering water by nasogastric tube. The reason is that the deficits are too severe and the rate of ongoing fluid losses exceeds the rate at which fluids can be effectively delivered by nasogastric tube. Furthermore, such cases also often exhibit severe intestinal stasis (poor motility) and dysfunction. Therefore, water administered by tube may remain in the stomach and fail to be reabsorbed or pass farther down the intestinal tract without being absorbed.

Moderate to severe dehydration requires intravenous fluid therapy in order to provide large quantities directly to the cardiovascular system without the need to be absorbed from the intestine (as would be necessary with water administered by a nasogastric tube). Intravenous catheters are placed in the horse's jugular vein on the neck. Catheters must be appropriately managed as complications such as inflammation and infection of the vessel and surrounding tissues can occur. In severe cases large-bore catheters can be placed in both sides of the neck (two catheters). This is usually done when rapid fluid therapy is needed to help correct dehydration and endotoxemia.

Severe dehydration in a horse with colic or diarrhea is highly associated with a number of significant electrolyte disturbances. This is one of the reasons that referral hospitals regularly evaluate blood parameters of horses exhibiting colic. The abnormalities may be mild to severe depending on the severity of the colic, its underlying cause, and the duration of the underlying cause. Even horses with mild or chronic colic may exhibit significant blood abnormalities, particularly if the duration of the underlying cause has been great. Evaluation of blood parameters will provide some information regarding the severity of endotoxemia and acid/base disturbances (if present). Frequently, horses with endotoxemia, severe colic, and/or diarrhea exhibit low blood sodium, low chloride, low potassium, and often low blood calcium levels. The acid-base evaluation most often reveals various degrees of acidosis (due to too much relative hydrogen ion). These abnormalities are generally attributable to the fluid and electrolyte loss into the intestinal tract (from the body). The fluid in the intestinal tract may accumulate in any number of areas and cause distension and pain. It is considered to be lost from the body once it enters the intestinal tract. Abnormal volumes of fluid may enter the intestinal tract with any intestinal upset. This fluid volume may overwhelm the normal absorptive function that recovers this fluid in the large intestine. The upset may also primarily affect the large intestine, rendering it incapable of reabsorbing the normal amount of fluid. Excess fluid in the large intestine that cannot be reabsorbed will be passed in the feces. This can produce loose feces or diarrhea. Excess fluid that accumulates in the small intestine or stomach is probably actively secreted into the intestine. It is lost usually through the reflux drawn off by the nasogastric tube. Fluid in the nasogastric reflux and in the feces takes with it large quantities of electrolytes. These electrolytes come from both lack of absorption by the dysfunctional intestine and by active secretion of water and electrolytes into the intestinal tract by inflamed and dysfunctional segments of intestine.

These imbalances continue until the intestine can resume adequate function to maintain them in the body (and not lose them into the intestine). Intravenous fluid therapy helps return and then maintain these levels and prevents complete loss of organ function until the intestinal tract can be either repaired surgically or "healed" with time and medical management. Severe dehydration, electrolyte, and/or acid-base disturbances can lead to death if they are not addressed and kept at levels adequate to prevent failure of organ function due to poor blood flow and inadequate levels of important electrolytes. Severe acidosis can lead to generalized biochemical dysfunction (enzyme activity and membrane stability of cells) of all organs and ultimately to death.

Other blood parameters that indicate poor hydration and tissue perfusion may include high creatinine and high blood lactate. Creatinine is a normal by-product of muscle metabolism. It becomes abnormally high in the blood when perfusion of the kidneys and, consequently, the elimination of creatinine is poor. Blood urea nitrogen (BUN) also increases due to poor blood flow to the kidneys. Persistent poor blood flow to the kidneys can lead to kidney damage. Blood lactate normally indicates anaerobic metabolism. In a normal horse with adequate blood flow, blood lactate is usually very low (unless the horse has undergone intense exercise). In a sick horse increases in blood lactate indicate poor tissue perfusion and, therefore, the need to burn energy without the presence of oxygen (since oxygenated blood supply to the tissue is poor).

### Additives to Intravenous Fluids/Rates of IV Fluid Administration

Several additives to the fluid are used to help maintain electrolyte levels at or near normal. The veterinarian will use the most beneficial type of commercially available fluid to help maintain hydration and electrolyte levels. Additives may be necessary if electrolytes that are abnormal on blood evaluations are either not present in the fluid bags or are too low in concentration to keep up with body demands and ongoing losses. The most commonly supplemented electrolytes in severely dehydrated and/or endotoxic horses include potassium chloride and calcium. Both of these electrolytes are important for numerous reasons but also have significant effects on intestinal motility. Low levels of each of these two electrolytes are highly associated with intestinal stasis, endotoxemia, and ongoing severe fluid and electrolyte losses.

Rates of intravenous fluid administration depend on the overall minute-to-minute stability of the horse. In severe acute situations, intravenous fluids are often delivered as fast as they will flow through the catheter or catheters. Once this fluid administration has clinically stabilized the horse, the rate is often decreased. Clinical improvement in hydration is determined by a return of blood flow as indicated by return of pink and moist mucous membrane color, adequate jugular vein refill, reduced heart rate, and increased urine production (blood flow to the kidney is returned). Re-establishment of blood parameters to normal also helps indicate rehydration and electrolyte balance. The packed cell volume (PCU) and total serum protein are easily performed and are helpful to evaluate and to follow patient hydration status. Fluid rates required for maintenance (normal body requirements only) are in the area of 1 milliliter per pound of body weight per hour (about 1 liter per hour for a 1,000-pound horse). However, this does not account for ongoing losses. Horses with diarrhea, significant gastric reflux, or other intestinal fluid loss will require higher rates of fluid administration to prevent dehydration and perpetual electrolyte and acid/base disturbances.

### Hypertonic Saline

In cases of severe dehydration, it may be necessary for a veterinarian to use two catheters to correct fluid losses more rapidly than even standard intravenous fluid administration permits. However, in some cases even this is too slow to meet the requirements for blood volume expansion in an emergency situation. In such a situation the horse is highly unstable and has life-threatening compromise to organ and tissue blood flow. Administration of hypertonic saline is a reasonable option for such patients. Usually about 1 to 2 liters of this solution are intravenously administered by rapid infusion. Hypertonic saline, because it is hypertonic (more concentrated than our own body blood and body fluids), rapidly exhibits osmotic draw of fluid from the horse's tissue into the vascular space. This quickly expands the lost circulating blood volume due to dehydration. Horses may benefit greatly and rapidly from this treatment in such situations. However, this treatment is like borrowing from a bank. The movement of fluid from the tissues into the vascular space provides tremendous immediate benefit; however, it depletes the body tissues of fluid. It helps to stabilize the patient rapidly but only temporarily. The volume of fluid "borrowed" from the tissues must be immediately replaced by intravenous fluid therapy or severe metabolic consequences will ensue in the tissues. The effects on the fluid shift to the vascular space is only transient — it buys some time for intravenous fluid therapy but does not replace the need for intravenous fluid therapy. Indeed, if the "borrowed" fluid is not paid back (with interest), the patient may subsequently destabilize to an even more severe state. Even so, hypertonic saline administration is often immediately life saving and permits the attending veterinarian time to get the intravenous fluids into the temporarily stabilized patient.

### Sodium Bicarbonate

Intravenous sodium bicarbonate administration is often used in horses to help correct severe acid/base imbalances, specifically acidosis. Bicarbonate deficits are usually calculated from the results of blood evaluations in order to administer the appropriate amount of bicarbonate to replenish that which is lost with intestinal fluid and to meet the amounts expected to be lost with ongoing intestinal upset and fluid loss. Sodium bicarbonate may be added to intravenous fluids, "piggy-backed" on the intravenous fluids through an injection port, or administered rapidly as an intravenous bolus. Horses that are acidotic are often afflicted with a number of other significant electrolyte imbalances and, therefore, are likely to require other electrolyte supplementation in their fluids and/or their water buckets.

Sodium bicarbonate is perhaps most frequently administered to horses that exhibit diarrhea. Often the diarrhea has been present for several days. Progressive loss of electrolytes and fluid volume in the diarrhea may lead to significant acidosis. Acidosis may be mild or severe. The underlying cause of the electrolyte and acid/base disturbance(s) is usually ongoing, and sodium bicarbonate administration may need to be repeated several times. As intestinal function returns, so too do the normal electrolyte values. As acid-base balance depends on electrolyte levels in the body, when the electrolyte values and hydration of the horse return to normal, so too does the acid/base balance. Normal pH of the blood is about 7.4. Acidosis is defined as blood pH of less than 7.35. In severe cases acidosis is life-threatening to the horse. Severe acidosis may be difficult to correct completely with sodium bicarbonate administration due to the difficulty in correcting immediate imbalances and the ability to keep up with ongoing losses. Sodium bicarbonate may be supplemented in the feed or water buckets of these patients but does not help if the horse is not eating or drinking.

### Albumin, Plasma, and Oxyglobin

These blood derivatives are often used in horses in replacement therapy for protein loss and/or for expansion of blood volume that helps "hold" the water component of the blood in the vascular space. Horses with diarrhea or other severe intestinal disturbances may become hypoproteinemic (develop low blood protein). The protein in the blood serves to help maintain the osmotic force (the draw and maintenance of the fluid volume in the blood vessels that prevent fluid leaking out of the blood vessels) in the blood and thus keep fluid volume within the vascular space. Excessive protein loss also causes the loss of this draw to some extent, and therefore the horse may lose the ability to maintain normal fluid volumes. Replacing protein with plasma or albumin will help combat the loss of the osmotic draw that should normally exist in the blood vessels. Low blood protein levels can cause a horse to become edematous and exhibit extensive swelling in the legs and along the belly and chest. Horses with low blood protein may also become unstable from inadequate circulating blood volumes. Because diarrhea is often associated with significant protein loss, horses that have diarrhea may be the most common adult recipients of plasma or other blood protein products. Administration of plasma to adult horses is expensive. They may require several liters on several occasions to help maintain blood protein levels, and each liter generally costs between $125 and $150 or more. Furthermore, horses that lose protein will also lose these blood products after they have been administered. Therefore, although this treatment does provide transient benefits, the administered protein may also eventually be lost and, therefore, require repeat administration.

Oxyglobin® (purified bovine hemoglobin) is a similar blood protein product but differs in that it can actually carry oxygen as well as provide increases in total protein blood levels. It, therefore, would also promote oxygen delivery to tissues, particularly helpful in patients suffering from inadequate blood volumes and tissue and organ perfusion (as is the case in endotoxemic horses). Unfortunately, at about $125 or more per 125 milliliters, it may be prohibitively expensive to use in adult horses. It has, however, been increasingly used in foals as their smaller size makes its use much more cost effective.

### Hetastarch

Hetastarch is a synthetic fluid replacement used extensively in human and equine medicine. It provides long-lasting blood volume expansion with reduced loss of fluid into the tissues from the blood vessels when compared to the amounts of fluid lost into the tissues when regular fluid therapy or plasma is used. The result of this is that hetastarch expands the fluid volume in the blood. Thus, the expansion of the fluid volume in the blood vessels occurs for a longer period. Hetastarch, also somewhat expensive, is used more extensively in foals than in adults. Nonetheless, several institutions use hetastarch for intravenous fluid replacement therapy in adults and foals. Very large doses may lead to bleeding disorders. The incidence of this in the horse has not been specifically addressed.

## ENEMAS: USEFUL?

Most impaction colic is associated with obstructions in the small and large intestines. Less commonly, impactions may occur in the small colon and rectum. Unless the impaction is in the small colon or rectum, the distance to the site of impaction is generally too far for an enema to be of benefit in an adult horse. Furthermore, introducing and pushing the large volume of fluid into the rectum with a tube or other device for delivery may be rather dangerous if not very carefully performed. Rectal tears are a very real concern with such therapy.

Foals are probably the most common equine recipients of enemas. These are often provided to help the foal pass its meconium (first manure) and to assist with the stimulation of intestinal motility via distension of the rectum and reflexive increase in intestinal motility in intestinal segments closer to the mouth. It is probably easiest and safest simply to use warm water and a mild soap (such as Ivory) at a volume of about 1/2 to 1 quart of water. Fleet enemas are commonly administered to foals without problem. However, equine neonatologists prefer not to use these prepared enemas due to their high phosphorous content. Enemas in foals should be used only if necessary and with great care, as rectal tears, rectal inflammation, and rectal strictures with subsequent motility disturbances can occur.

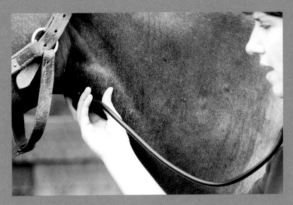

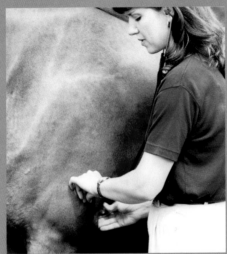

The colic exam includes taking the respiratory and heart rates as well as the temperature.

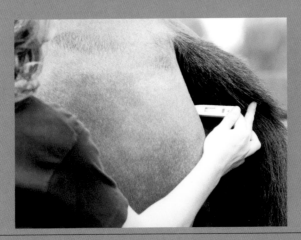

Part of the colic examination includes the "tent" test
in which the horse is checked for dehydration (above left and right)
and the capillary refill test (below left).
The horse in the lower right-hand photo displays
toxic mucous membranes.

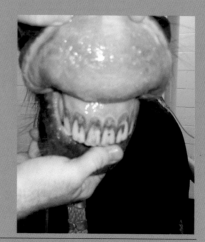

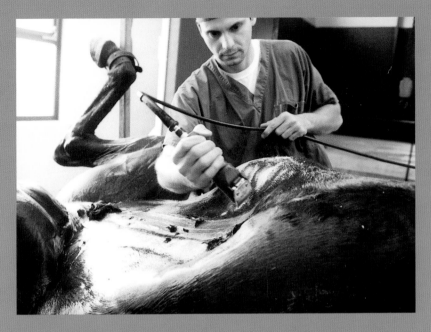

Preparing for colic surgery: clipping the abdomen (above),
disinfecting (below left), and checking vital signs.

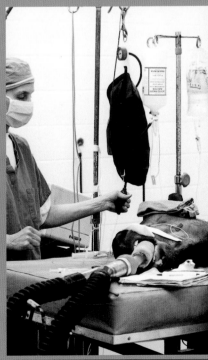

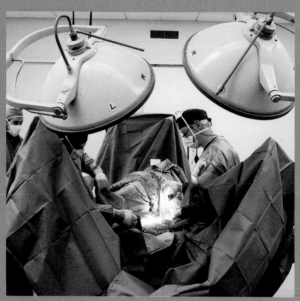

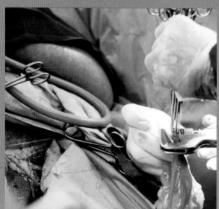

Surgeons open the abdomen (above), use a stapler while working on a section of intestine (left), and suture the affected area.

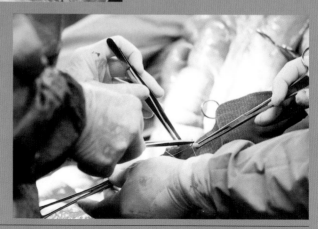

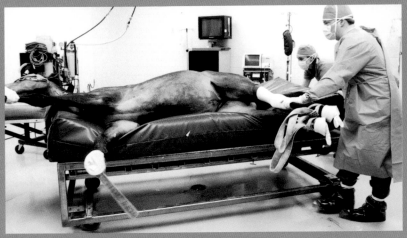

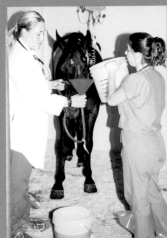

A horse is taken to a recovery stall
after surgery (above);
a nasogastric tube is used (right)
to flush a horse's stomach
after surgery. A colic patient
receives intravenous fluids (below).

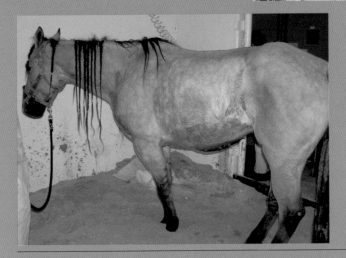

133

A muzzle helps restrict oral feed intake (above); a surgical wound dehiscence, or breakdown (below).

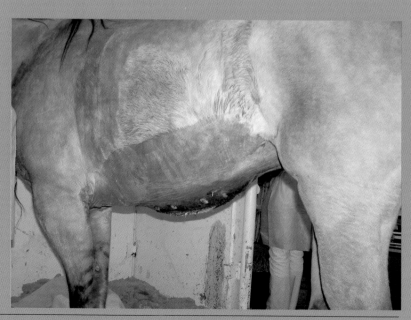

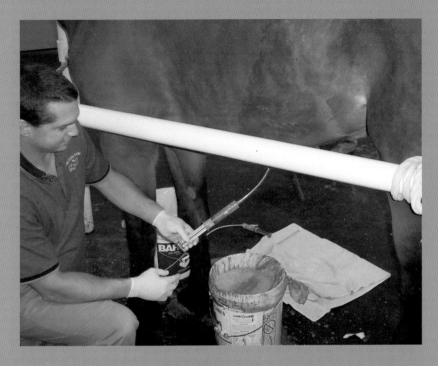

Draining an abdominal abscess (above); checking on a post-surgical
patient (below).

Horses that live in stalls can be more prone
to colic than those that can forage at liberty.
Colic prevention should include regular dental care
and deworming (below).

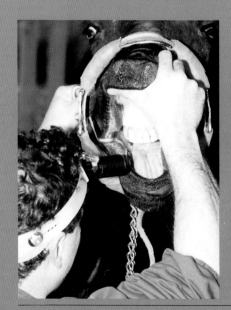

Foals that experience meconium impaction may be treated rectally with retention enemas consisting of acetylcysteine as a 4% solution, and delivered by a catheter with an inflatable cuff so the foal retains the solution for 20 minutes or more. The premise of this therapy is similar to that of DSS in that the acetylcysteine serves to destroy some of the cohesive bonding on the impaction surface and loosen and lubricate it.

## ENDOTOXEMIA: DEFINITION AND ANTI-ENDOTOXIN THERAPY

Endotoxin, the culprit in the syndrome known as endotoxemia, is a cell wall constituent of gram-negative bacteria capable of producing severe and acute inflammatory and cardiovascular destabilization in any patient. Endotoxin is released from these bacteria when they either die or grow very rapidly. Endotoxemia begins when endotoxin finds its way into the circulation in levels that cannot be "detoxified" by the liver. This occurs when the intestinal barrier is compromised. Such compromise probably occurs either by intestinal strangulation and cessation of blood supply to the area or by other intestinal disorders that lead to poor blood flow and disruption of normal structure and function of intestinal tissue. Endotoxin's entrance into the circulation can trigger an extensive series of biochemical events that results in massive release of inflammatory mediators from numerous types of cells. These inflammatory mediators lead to the overall destabilization of the cardiovascular system, the blood clotting mechanisms, and other organ systems, a response known as systemic inflammatory response syndrome (SIRS). Endotoxemia does not occur in all colic cases. Indeed, usually only the more severe cases of colic and diarrhea tend to be complicated by endotoxemia.

Because the body's response to endotoxin is complex, no single therapy is likely to act as a "silver bullet" to halt and/or prevent the response to endotoxin (SIRS). Therefore, there are numerous proposed treatments to help combat endotoxemia. Some treatments must be used within a specific time period to have any helpful effects. For instance, plasma (J5 plasma) that is rich in endotoxin-specific antibodies has been used to capture endotoxin by directly binding to it before it can interact with inflammatory cells and to promote endotoxin removal from the circulation. However, this therapy is obviously ineffective if the endotoxin has already engaged inflammatory cells and elicited their response, and, therefore, highly time-dependent. Nonetheless, this therapy may help prevent further effects of endotoxin on inflammatory cells and may be used for several consecutive days when endotoxemia is likely to be persistent. Plasma also is rich in other helpful factors such as protein, helpful control agents of inflammation, clotting factors, and inhibitors of over-active clotting tendencies that may occur with endotoxemia. For this reason alone, both regular plasma and J5 plasma may help control and manage endotoxemia.

Anti-inflammatory drugs, particularly the non-steroidal anti-inflammatory drugs (NSAIDs), are commonly used to help manage and control the effects of endotoxemia. Flunixin meglumine (Banamine®) is probably the most commonly used NSAID to help control the signs associated with endotoxemia. This drug has been shown to help decrease the production of some of the inflammatory mediators and to control other deleterious effects of substances released in response to endotoxin. Although there are other NSAIDs, research and clinical experience indicate that flunixin meglumine is more effective in the control and treatment of the effects of endotoxemia. "Low-dose" flunixin meglumine is commonly used and is effective at suppressing the production of inflammatory products and mediators. Flunixin meglumine is commonly administered to post-operative colic cases and to horses with diarrhea. Ketoprofen (Ketofen®) has also been used to help combat endotoxemia. Ketoprofen is believed to be less likely to cause intestinal ulceration than other NSAIDs. However, ketoprofen may not be as good at controlling pain as flunixin meglumine.

Polymixin B is an aminoglycoside antibiotic that has been extensively investigated in human medicine for apparent anti-endotoxic effects that are unrelated to its antibiotic activity. For horses, polymixin B is often added to a 1-liter bag of intravenous fluid and administered once to twice a day. Because it is potentially toxic to the kidneys, polymixin B cannot be used in horses that exhibit kidney damage or poor blood flow to the kidneys. Polymixin B binds to circulating endotoxin and thereby may help to decrease the effects of endotoxin on the animal.

Dimethylsulfoxide (DMSO) may be used to help combat the effects of endotoxemia. This compound is usually administered on the basis of its ability to scavenge damaging inflammatory free radicals. DMSO is also believed to have a primary anti-inflammatory effect and to protect cell membrane integrity. When applied to a specific region of the body, it has been suggested to increase blood flow. It is unknown if such an effect may occur with systemic administration of this compound. DMSO is usually given intravenously as a 10% to 20% solution. It must be given in dilution to prevent breakdown or other damage to red blood cells. DMSO is highly absorbed through most membranes. For this reason it can also be administered by nasogastric tube.

Pentoxyfilline (Trental®) is gaining increasing attention for its effectiveness in combating endotoxemia. Research has indicated that pentoxyfilline appears to suppress a major inflammatory mediator and, therefore, may provide clinical benefit to horses with endotoxemia. It also improves red blood cell deformability (makes the cells more elastic and "stretchy") and causes vasodilation. The effects of this drug on the cardiovascular system may make it beneficial for the treatment of laminitis and endotoxemia. However, one investigation indicated little beneficial effect of pentoxyfilline when administered intravenously to horses challenged with endotoxin.

*Salmonella typhimurium* antiserum is commercially produced to help combat endotoxemia. The benefits of its administration are not restricted to diseases caused by *Salmonella* species. The antiserum may be effective at decreasing the effects of endotoxin by direct binding and subsequent removal from circulation.

## PROKINETICS (DRUGS THAT STIMULATE INTESTINAL MOTILITY)

Under certain circumstances a clinician will have to consider therapy that helps improve intestinal motility. Most commonly, such therapy is instituted after abdominal surgery in the horse. Post-operative ileus (poor intestinal motility) is relatively common, particularly for colic surgery. However, inflammatory conditions may also produce poor intestinal motility. Anterior enteritis (inflammation of the small intestinal segment closest to the stomach) is a specific condition commonly associated with poor intestinal motility. Inflammation of the abdominal cavity (peritonitis) may also lead to generalized reduction of intestinal motility. Drugs used to promote intestinal motility may directly stimulate smooth muscle contraction of the intestine or may act by indirectly moderating the negative effects of inflammation on intestinal motility.

Drugs that directly affect intestinal smooth muscle contraction generally act through the intestinal nervous system by stimulating the effects of acetylcholine. Acetylcholine is a neurotransmitter agent in the intestinal nervous system. As a neurotransmitter, it is a substance that is released by nerve cells to stimulate intestinal motility.

Neostigmine is a drug that reduces the breakdown of acetylcholine and, therefore, lets it "accumulate" in the intestine so it can stimulate more intestinal motility. Its effects only last 10 to 15 minutes, and it often requires multiple daily doses. Despite its apparent benefits in promoting intestinal motility, neostigmine tends to increase disorganized intestinal contractions. Therefore, it may actually decrease progressive motility of the small intestine and delay gastric emptying. It may cause further abdominal pain by inducing spasmodic contractions. Through a different mechanism than that exhibited by neostigmine, metaclopramide also serves to stimulate the activity of the intestinal nervous system by increasing the release of acetylcholine. Metaclopramide is often delivered as an infusion over a one-hour period but is associated with a high rate of undesirable central nervous system side effects. Domperidone acts in a similar manner but does not cross the blood-brain barrier in the doses used to promote intestinal motility. It is believed to be potentially useful for post-operative ileus and may have significant potential for clinical use. Cisapride also enhances acetylcholine release. It supports gastric emptying, jejunal motility, and colonic motility and increases the coordination of progressive intestinal motility. This drug's promotion of motility may affect intestinal segments from the mouth to the anus. This medication is no longer available in injectable form but does exist in tablet form. However, horses that are refluxing are probably poor candidates for any oral medication. This drug has been administered rectally to horses with anecdotal reports of clinical success, but studies failed to show any significant absorption.

Erythromycin lactobionate is an antibiotic that appears to exhibit some activity as a motility-enhancing agent for ileus. It appears to promote acetylcholine release in the intestinal nervous system by still another mechanism. Frequently, this drug is diluted in 1 liter of saline or other fluid and infused over one hour up to four times a day. High doses of this drug may actually harm intestinal motility. Repeat usage may lead to reduced sensitivity of the receptors to the effects of this drug. Careful and judicious use and administration are warranted because this drug is associated with the development of diarrhea in horses.

Acepromazine and yohimbine are drugs with alpha-adrenergic antagonistic properties. They are used on the premise that sympathetic nervous system hyperactivity may contribute to ileus (poor intestinal motility) by inhibiting the release of the intestinal nervous system neurotransmitter, acetylcholine. Acepromazine and yohimbine have both been shown to be potentially beneficial in managing post-operative ileus. Yohimbine may be more effective when used in combination with bethanecol. Acepromazine must not be used for analgesia (because it provides no pain-killing effect) and cannot be administered safely to a dehydrated animal since it causes vasodilation and rapid reduction in blood pressure, which could be life-threatening in such horses.

Bethanecol directly acts on smooth muscle to induce contraction. In experimental models it has been shown to improve gastrointestinal motility. Side effects including colic, diarrhea, and salivation may occur with bethanecol; therefore, it requires judicious use.

Lidocaine has already been described as a potential drug used in pain management. However, it is also used for its proposed motility enhancement and anti-inflammatory properties. It may be effective in helping to control damage to tissue from the reintroduction of oxygen to oxygen-deprived intestinal tissue. It has motility-enhancing effects that may be due largely to these characteristics. This drug is delivered as an intravenous bolus and then followed by continuous infusion at a reduced dosage rate. Toxic side effects relating to the central nervous system are also possible, especially if the medication is delivered too rapidly.

Although it may seem empirical that all horses that experience colic have poor intestinal motility and should receive motility-enhancing drugs, this is far from the case. Indeed, appropriate use of motility-enhancing medications will realistically apply to a very small number of horses that experience colic. Horses that receive motility-enhancing medications appropriately are most often being treated for either post-operative ileus or anterior enteritis. Horses with colic due to undefined or undiagnosed conditions, impactions, or other obstructions are *not* candidates for such medications because of the potential for intestinal rupture or exacerbation of the underlying condition(s). Administration of motility drugs may be associated with numerous side effects. Therefore, horses receiving such medications must be closely monitored for clinical effects and signs of toxicity. Because of these requirements, their use should probably be restricted to a hospital environment with intensive care and monitoring for these patients.

## NON-SURGICAL MANIPULATIONS UNDER GENERAL ANESTHESIA

A few specific causes of acute abdominal pain can be addressed by non-surgical manipulations performed while the horse is under general anesthesia. Such causes include nephrosplenic entrapment, uterine torsion, and dystocia. For these conditions, manipulations that might correct the problem without surgery require the ability to turn and roll the body of the recumbent horse. Nephrosplenic entrapment may be corrected by anesthetizing the horse, placing it in right lateral recumbency, and rolling the horse over to the left side. The horse is usually shaken and rolled back and forth to help dislodge the entrapped colon from the nephrosplenic ligament.

Uterine torsion also may be corrected non-surgically with the aid of general anesthesia by one of two techniques: "planking the flank" or manual rotation of the uterus and the foal through the cervix of the mare. The horse is evaluated for the direction of the uterine torsion and under general anesthesia is placed in recumbency with the spine to the floor. For the "planking the flank" technique, a large wooden plank is placed across the abdomen and weight applied on its ends. The horse is then rolled in the opposite direction of the torsion while the board "holds" the uterus in place. This procedure may effectively reduce a uterine torsion without surgery. Trans-cervical manipulations may be performed under general anesthesia to de-rotate the torsed uterus as well. Finally, dystocia also may be successfully managed using general anesthesia, placing of the mare's hind limbs in hobbles, and lifting her back end. This often removes much of the effects of gravity and abdominal organs on the space within the uterus, allowing much greater manipulation of the foal in the uterus and permitting correction of the displaced foal to allow vaginal delivery.

One must understand that these non-surgical procedures are far from universally successful and not appropriate for all situations. In many instances these problems cannot be corrected using these methods and will therefore require surgery. For instance, if a dystocia has continued for several hours, it may be unreasonable to try non-surgical manipulations to remove the foal since the foal is likely to be significantly compromised by that time. It may not be in the foal's best interest to realize at this point that non-surgical correction won't work because wasted time will impose further danger to the foal. Attending veterinarians must have some experience with such non-surgical procedures and have access to necessary equipment, such as a hoist and hobbles, for such manipulations to have a chance of succeeding.

## SURGERY AS THERAPEUTIC INTERVENTION

Most of the time, whenever a horse goes to surgery for colic, the surgery is both diagnostic and (hopefully) therapeutic. Exploratory surgery is most often performed by a midline incision on the abdomen, extending from the area of the umbilicus forward. Such an approach is more common than laparoscopic surgery for two reasons: it permits better visualization and access to the abdomen and it allows for better manipulation and exteriorization of intestine, permitting correction of the underlying condition. Indeed, the laparoscopic surgical procedure is far more valuable as a diagnostic tool than as a therapeutic procedure. This stems from the size of the equine abdomen and the very small window provided by the laparoscope for both visualization and especially for manipulations.

Most surgical approaches will be performed from a midline

incision to permit the best exposure and maneuverability for the necessary interventions. The most common surgical interventions in acute colic cases probably include surgical resection of non-viable or questionably viable intestine, enterotomy (incision into the intestine) to remove obstructions such as foreign bodies and fecal and other impactions, removal of sand from the intestine, removal of enteroliths (a rock that forms in the intestine), surgical opening of constricted or scarred areas, and breakdown of adhesions (scar tissue bands). Another common surgical intervention follows intestinal resection. This involves reconnection of the remaining viable ends of intestine (after the non-viable section has been removed), termed anastomosis.

The final step of any abdominal surgery is closing the abdomen. The technique often depends on the individual surgeon's preferences, but generally it includes closure of the linea alba with very heavy absorbable suture, closure of the subcutaneous layers with much more fine, absorbable suture, and finally skin closure using staples or a non-absorbable suture.

## CHAPTER 5

# On-Farm Management of Horses with Colic

To some extent, on-farm management of horses with acute abdominal pain is limited by equipment, time constraints, and availability of specialized personnel. Your veterinarian must evaluate each case individually and determine the most reasonable approach for the initial management of the patient. A veterinarian experienced in handling colic can perform many therapies on the farm. However, from the previous descriptions, it is obvious that many more intensive therapies are either impractical or impossible on the farm. Therapies most commonly instituted on the farm include administration of pain medications, passage of a nasogastric tube to check reflux, administration of various compounds by nasogastric tube (such as mineral oil, magnesium sulfate, etc.), restriction of feed intake, dietary changes, and deworming. Less commonly used therapies that may be instituted at the farm include periodic refluxing by nasogastric tube (ever hour to every several hours), intravenous fluid therapy (continuous or a large volume administered at one time), trocharizatrion (placement of a needle through the body wall and into gas-distended intestine to relieve the gas and pain associated with the distension), general anesthesia, "rolling" (anesthetizing and physically rolling the horse's body to correct a specific type of intestinal displacement), and administration, near the tail-head, of pain-killing drugs into a space that overlies the spinal cord (epidural).

On occasion a veterinarian may not be readily available or an owner may live a great distance from a veterinarian. Managing such a colic situation requires substantial planning, especially for those who live far from any available veterinarian or veterinary service. Horses without readily available veterinary attention should be given excellent health care and management to minimize the risk

## AT A GLANCE

• Administering pain medication is one of the most common colic therapies instituted on the farm.

• Owners should consult with their veterinarians before giving a horse any pain medication.

• Take time to form a plan for colic and other emergencies.

of acute and chronic colic. However, if a horse in this situation shows evidence of acute abdominal pain, it is important to recognize the signs early to maximize the likelihood of a successful outcome. Owners of such animals can begin by walking the horse to help minimize the perception of abdominal pain and possibly help stimulate intestinal motility. Horses whose pain cannot be controlled by walking should probably receive pain medication.

Owners who live far from veterinary services should keep at hand a small supply of medications, including pain medications. It is ideal, though sometimes impossible, to discuss on the phone with a veterinarian the appropriate type of medication, dosage, and other uses of pain medications. Flunixin meglumine (Banamine®) is probably appropriate at the outset of a colic episode. A 1,000- to 1,100-pound horse should receive about 500 milligrams (10 cc) of this medication either in the jugular vein or in the muscle. The onset of the medication's activity is much more rapid when it is administered IV. If flunixin meglumine is not available, ketoprofen or phenylbutazone may be used. Ketoprofen may be administered into a vein or into the muscle. The dose is also 1 gram (1,000 mg), or 10 cc.

Injectable phenylbutazone *can only be given intravenously*. The IV formulation acts more quickly than its oral counterpart. This drug causes severe tissue damage if delivered outside of a vein. The intravenous dose is between 1 and 2 grams (5 to 10 cc), depending on severity of pain. Intravenous injections in the horse should only be administered by people trained and skilled in their administration. Phenylbutazone, as an oral medication, should not be used in situations that require rapid pain-killing effects. It will not exhibit significant pain-killing effects for over an hour. Furthermore, if the intestine is dysfunctional, normal absorption of the drug may not occur.

Overall, it is generally believed that flunixin meglumine is superior to other NSAID medications for colic. Therefore, a horse owner who lives far from a veterinarian should probably purchase a bottle of injectable flunixin meglumine.

Administration of any pain medication will be most appropriately performed and safest if the owner consults a veterinarian by phone or otherwise. Horses that display persistent pain may benefit from a repeat dose of flunixin meglumine; however, the need for any repeat medication, especially when pain relief only lasts a short time (less than one hour) could signal the need for more intensive veterinary intervention. Severe pain is often associated with more severe underlying conditions.

If a horse requires immediate pain relief due to violent colic (manifest by relentless moving, pawing, getting up and down, and rolling), more potent and faster-acting pain medications than the NSAIDs will be required. Some farm managers and experienced horse owners may have one of the alpha-adrenergic agonist drugs on hand, particularly xylazine (Rompun®). If this is the case and there is no available veterinary service or consultation, xylazine may be administered intravenously at a dose of about 150 milligrams to 250 milligrams per 1,000-pound horse. For commercially available formulations that are 100 milligrams per milliliter, this is 1 1/2 to 2 1/2 cc intravenously. The same medication may be used in the muscle, but intramuscular administration will preclude rapid onset of pain relief. If such medication is required for pain relief, a veterinarian should examine the horse as soon as possible.

Detomidine (Dormosedan®) is another alpha-adrenergic agonist that should only be handled by veterinarians and highly experienced caretakers. This drug is more potent and tends to have longer-lasting effects than xylazine. Usually only about 5 to 7.5 milligrams (1/2 to 3/4 of a cc) of detomidine intravenously is adequate for immediate pain relief. Again, if you are using this drug, the horse needs to be examined by a veterinarian.

Some horses suffering significant colic may improve with a trailer ride, but never rely on a trailer ride to "fix" your horse. Many owners and trainers have noted an apparent association between having loaded and driven a horse in the trailer to the hospital and a resolution of the abdominal pain by the time the horse arrives. Although it is always theoretically possible for a piece of displaced and distended intestine to return to its normal location and size during a trailer ride, it is probably more likely that horses with abdominal pain that improve by the end of a trailer ride were likely to improve anyway. Nonetheless, many horse owners and trainers insist on considering a trailer ride as a potential therapeutic intervention. If a trailer ride is in the management plan for a colic, it should be so only under one of two conditions: 1) the trailer ride is en route to a clinic or referral hospital, or 2) there is no option of surgery for the horse. A trailer ride as a therapeutic intervention that is not en route to a surgical facility otherwise wastes highly valuable time and may decrease the chance of survival of a horse that requires surgery.

Other worthwhile practices for on-farm management of colic include immediate removal of all feed and hay, recording or noting the amount of fecal production, and confining the horse to the stall. It will be helpful to your veterinarian if you learn to obtain a heart rate from your horse before any emergencies ever occur. This enables you to ascertain a heart rate during emergency situations and to share it with your veterinarian. The heart rate can usually be easily obtained using a hand to feel the heartbeat on the left side of the chest or, even better, a stethoscope directly behind the left elbow on the chest of the horse. The heart rate should be counted for at least 15 seconds and multiplied by four to provide a heart rate per minute. Keep in mind that there are at least two heart sounds to be heard, the "lub" and the "dub," that constitute one contraction of the heart. Practice taking your horse's heart rate before an emergency situation requires it. The normal heart rate of a horse varies between 36 and 44 beats per minute. Horses that are experiencing mild pain may exhibit heart rates between 48 and 52 beats per minute. Moderate pain may produce a heart rate of 60 to 70, and more severe pain is often associated with heart rates greater than 80 beats per minute. Remember there are other things that can affect the heart rate, so take the horse's behavior into consideration. A horse with a heart rate of 80 beats or more that is standing quietly probably has something in addition to pain affecting the heart rate. Have a rectal thermometer available. Provide your veterinarian with an accurate reading of your horse's rectal temperature to help him/her assess your horse more rapidly and completely. Your veterinarian will probably repeat these procedures. This is not because he/she does not believe what you told him, but more because trends of heart rate and temperature will provide more information on what is happening in your horse during a colic episode.

It is not necessary to keep a horse from lying down unless it is rolling. If the horse is rolling, the horse should be walked and probably receive pain medication until the veterinarian can come. If the horse is lying quietly, allow it to do so. The colic episode may fatigue the horse. Monitor the horse closely and get him up only if he begins to show continued signs of distress such as rolling. Horses that exhibit colic and fluid coming from the nose should have both feed and water removed. This may be an indication of severe gastric reflux or of an esophageal obstruction (choke). Such animals should receive no food or water and should receive a veterinarian exam as soon as possible. Horses should never be "tubed" (pass a nasogastric tube) by anyone other than a veterinarian or a qualified and appropriately trained veterinary technician. An improperly performed nasogastric tubing can lead to several potentially life-threatening complications.

An emergency situation that requires a nasogastric tube is not the time to realize that arrangements for emergency care have not been addressed. Such poor planning often leads to panic on the part of those involved, and emergency situations are not well managed under the added stress of panic. Take time to formulate a plan for colics and other emergencies. Have phone numbers readily posted and easily accessible. Contact your designated veterinarian and get an idea of how long it will take him/her to reach your farm. If you cannot get the services of a veterinarian, make some arrangements for shipping your horse to an accessible facility or contact a small animal or mixed animal veterinarian and make some arrangements for such emergency situations. Don't wait until an emergency occurs before you think about how it will be managed and treated.

Horses in extreme pain can thrash violently, posing a danger to themselves and anyone around them. They should be handled only by experienced personnel. If veterinary assistance is not immediately available, the horse should be carefully and safely sedated using heavy doses of a potent sedative agent, such as xylazine or detomidine. If no pain medications are available and/or there is no way to approach the horse in a reasonably safe manner, the horse should be left alone to minimize potential human injuries. If severe pain persists and/or the horse continues to injure itself, it becomes a candidate for euthanasia.

# CHAPTER 6

## Making the Decision for Surgery

The decision to send a horse to surgery cannot be taken lightly. Such a decision must weigh the pros and cons of performing abdominal surgery. Because emergency or even routine abdominal surgery in an adult horse is not cheap, financial factors often enter into the decision-making process. Although not all horses are appropriate candidates for colic surgery and the economics of horse ownership often demand that an owner not spend more money on the animal than its innate value, we also must recognize we have some responsibility for their appropriate care and quality of life. As such, we should practice good health care for our horses to maintain quality of life and to avoid situations that lend themselves to emergency episodes.

In devising and meeting this level of care, we should also have thought about and planned for an emergency colic and for the need of emergency abdominal surgery. The horse owner should be aware of the cost of abdominal surgery and be prepared for dealing with such a situation before it occurs. In ownership and management of horses, it is probably better to own fewer horses and care for them better than to own more horses and cut back on their health care needs. Indeed, poor health care lends itself to more emergency situations that ultimately cost more money. The outcomes of emergency situations also tend to be poorer because the pre-planning has not included management of such situations.

Colic surgery is not cheap. Typical but uncomplicated colic surgery costs vary but probably range from $3,000 to $7,000 or more. More complicated surgeries incur greater expenses. Greater expense comes not only from the increased complexity of the surgery itself (e.g., intestinal resections), but also from more prolonged and intensive requirements for post-operative care. Horses with severe conditions, more extensive colic surgeries, and more intensive

> ## AT A GLANCE
>
> • When deciding on colic surgery, owners should consider their horse's condition and age, the overall costs, and the severity of the colic episode.
>
> • Even if the need for surgery is unclear, it is better to ship the horse to a surgical facility as a precaution.
>
> • Most colic surgeries are exploratory because a specific diagnosis can be difficult to determine.

post-operative care (e.g., large colon volvulus) may incur much larger bills, perhaps in excess of $10,000.

Many equine insurance companies offer major medical insurance that can include major medical and surgical coverage in addition to the more common mortality coverage. The required minimum mortality coverage may be as low as $5,000, an amount that usually is associated with relatively reasonable premiums. Major medical and surgical coverage is often easily added to the premium at affordable premiums.

Time is of the essence if your horse has a surgical lesion. The affected intestinal segment can die quickly, requiring its surgical removal (resection). Horses that undergo resections and horses with poorly viable intestine confront more post-operative complications and have an overall poorer prognosis. If you don't live near a referral (surgical) facility, you should plan to refer your horse earlier than other owners. However, if your horse is not a candidate for emergency colic surgery (due to advanced age, financial constraints, unrelated health problems, or other reasons), this preparation will not be an issue. If your horse is a surgical candidate, then it is more prudent to refer the horse earlier rather than later. In many instances it can be unclear for some time whether a colicky horse will require surgery. For owners who live far from surgical facilities, this is not time to waste because if the horse does wind up requiring surgery, the intestine can become unhealthy by the time that surgery becomes clearly necessary. If the horse has not already been shipped to the surgery facility, the intestine will probably be non-viable by the time the abdomen is opened. Therefore, though it might be unclear if surgery will be necessary, it is probably prudent to ship such horses immediately to prevent the lost time that will contribute to serious intestinal compromise.

The decision to operate is usually based on numerous and repetitive clinical evaluations of the horse. Much of the decision comes from the attending veterinarian's experience combined with the horse's clinical signs. Major findings that are considered potential indications for surgery include persistent pain despite pain-killing medication, persistently high heart rates, rectal exam findings that may indicate a surgical problem, copious reflux from the nasogastric tube, increased protein and inflammatory cells in the abdominal fluid, recurrent episodes of colic, ultrasound findings suggestive of a surgical problem, and lack of response to medical management of recurrent colic.

Because the decision for surgery is often unclear, the surgical approach is often described as "exploratory." Exploration of the abdomen in search of a potential cause of the abdominal pain is a diagnostic procedure. Exploratory surgeries in which nothing abnormal is identified are not wasted procedures. Such exploration, though not definitively diagnostic, does tell the surgeon what the horse does not have. Therefore, no further confusion exists as to whether the horse suffers from a lesion that requires surgical intervention.

## PREPARING TO SHIP TO A REFERRAL FACILITY

Once you have developed a plan for emergency situations, you should also consider the requirements for rapid and safe transport of your horse to the referral institution of your choice. This means coordinating with your regular veterinarian to contact the referral center as rapidly as possible once a decision for referral is made. Either you or your veterinarian should contact the referral hospital to provide the necessary information. This information probably will include the following:

• the name, age, breed, and sex of the horse

• the history of the problem (duration of colic, degree of pain exhibited, response to therapies that may have been provided, etc.)

• diagnostics that have been performed (results of the physical examination, rectal examination findings, and laboratory work)

• any and all treatments that have been and/or are being administered

• estimated time of arrival to the referral hospital

• contact phone numbers (especially any mobile phone numbers of the person[s] transporting the horse, the owner's contact numbers where he/she can be reached immediately during evaluation at the referral hospital, the referring veterinarian's name, contact address, and phone number[s])

• surgical candidacy of the horse (willingness to spend money on surgery or feasibility for surgery regarding age of horse and current physical status)

• plan for financial responsibilities

• the name and contact information of the insurance company (if any).

Horses being transported for surgery should be prepared. Protective clothing, headgear, and leg wraps may be warranted if these precautions can be easily and rapidly applied. Such items may help reduce trauma from shipping and thrashing during the transport, but extensive amounts of time should not be spent in applying such gear. Many horses that are being referred are dehydrated. When necessary, intravenous fluids can accompany the horse. Continuous administration of fluids during transport requires placing an intravenous catheter within one or both of the jugular veins. Horses in pain will also require some reliable pain management. In more severe colic cases, such pain relief does not last indefinitely. Therefore, your veterinarian may need to select more potent pain medications and provide pre-measured syringes of pain medication for repeat doses that may be needed during transport. Overall, the goals for transport to a referral facility are to get the horse there as quickly, safely, and comfortably as possible.

## SURGERY

As stated previously, it is often unclear if a particular horse experiencing a colic episode will require surgical intervention. When this is the case and especially when the nearest hospital is far away, it is probably safest to send the horse earlier rather than later. A colicky horse might actually improve with a trailer ride, and the initial evaluation at a referral facility may not yield enough specific information to warrant surgery. Often in such a situation, the attending veterinarian(s) could decide to "wait and watch." This is a reasonable approach when the horse is not in intractable pain and/or when there is an index of suspicion that the horse could be affected by a non-surgical type of colic episode. However, the return of abdominal pain during the "wait and watch" period often indicates the need for surgical intervention. Such a decision is never absolute, but again, the safest approach may be to opt for surgery earlier rather than later. The findings considered by most equine surgeons in assessing the need for surgical intervention include the following:
- degree of abdominal pain
- heart rate trends

• rectal examination findings

• amount of and character of reflux from the nasogastric tube and response of heart rate to relieving stomach fluid (reflux)

• evaluation of the abdominal fluid (cell count, types and protein levels)

• overall patient stability as indicated by the physical examination

• results of blood analysis

• degree of dehydration

• presence or absence of a fever.

## THE EXPLORATORY ABDOMINAL SURGERY

Nearly all colic surgeries are exploratory because the specific diagnosis is often unclear to the surgical team. Even when there is fairly strong evidence of a specific diagnosis, the surgeon might discover another problem or additional abnormalities once surgery is under way. Assuming that immediate surgery is necessary, preparation of the horse at the referral hospital will begin immediately when the decision is made. In the case of a horse with chronic or mild intermittent colic, surgery might be postponed if the horse is stable and has had the condition for an extended period. Such postponement permits elective exploratory surgery during regular hospital hours. This avoids the after-hours emergency fees and the need to call in and pay a surgical team, often making the procedure substantially less expensive.

Horses being prepared for exploratory surgery usually undergo certain basic preparations. These often include preliminary complete blood count and serum biochemical analysis. Such evaluations add much to the information of the current health status of the horse as it enters surgery. The anesthetist frequently uses this information in predicting the needs of the anesthetized horse for maintaining blood pressure, ventilation, and perfusion of organs. Other preparations prior to entry into the stall for induction of anesthesia include the placement of an intravenous catheter in one or both jugular veins for continual fluid administration, preoperative antibiotic administration (often potassium penicillin and gentamicin), and final refluxing by nasogastric tube. Nasogastric intubation immediately prior to surgery can minimize the likelihood of aspiration of gastric contents while the horse is turned on its back, reduce the pressure of a full stomach against the diaphragm, reduce pressure of the stomach contents on the major veins that return blood to the heart, and minimize the inhibition of ventilatory movements of the diaphragm. The horse's mouth is often flushed prior to induction of anesthesia.

Once the preparations have been completed, the horse is walked into an induction area and/or stall. Most horses receive further sedation prior to anesthetic induction. The injectable anesthetic agent is then administered through the catheter in the jugular vein. This medication is often ketamine and can be mixed with another drug called guaifenesin (a.k.a. GG), a muscle-relaxing agent. The horse is gently leaned against a padded wall and, as the anesthetics begin to work, is eased to the floor against the padded wall.

Before the horse is hoisted onto the table, an endotracheal tube is placed through the mouth and into the trachea. This is necessary because it is impractical and dangerous to use only injectable anesthetic agents to maintain anesthesia for the duration of a colic surgery. Inhaled agents, including halothane, isoflurane, and sevoflurane, are used to sustain anesthesia because they are safer and more sparing of blood pressure, ventilation, and tissue perfusion over longer periods. Once the endotracheal tube is placed and its cuff inflated, it is connected to an anesthesia machine capable of allowing the horse to breathe on its own or capable of mechanically administering the breaths as controlled by the anesthetist. The anesthesia machine is equipped with a "vaporizer" that permits the anesthetist to mix the inhaled air with a dialed concentration of the inhalant anesthetic agent.

Through clinical evaluation of the depth of anesthesia, the anesthetist determines the concentrations. Higher percentages of inhalant lead to deeper planes of anesthesia. Once the anesthesia machine is connected, the anesthetist usually places leads for continuous heart monitoring by an ECG. Most referral facilities also place arterial catheters, usually in a facial artery, through which they directly monitor blood pressures during surgery.

The surgical team then becomes very busy with numerous simultaneous tasks. Often, the horse's shoes are pulled to minimize damage to expensive recovery stall floors and to minimize the possibility of the horse's sustaining injury during recovery. The team often places hobbles below the fetlocks in order to hoist the horse onto the surgical table. The surgery table usually has very large mats or inflatable cushions to help minimize possible muscle damage while the horse is in recumbency. Once the horse is on the table, the surgical team begins to clip and scrub the abdomen.

When clipping and initial scrubbing are completed, the horse is transported into the surgery room on the surgery table. At this time the surgeon and assistant surgeon(s) leave to scrub themselves and don surgical garb. A surgery technician begins a final sterile scrub of the abdomen while the anesthetist finishes his/her preparations. The surgeons work together to place sterile drapes over the horse's abdomen with a centrally located opening through which the abdominal incision is made.

The abdominal incision is made directly on midline extending from near the umbilicus toward the head. The length of the incision varies, depending on the surgeon. However, the incision might need to be extended farther toward the head to facilitate more complete access to the abdominal contents.

## THE EXPLORATORY SURGICAL DIAGNOSIS

When the abdomen is opened, the surgeons go through a

routine evaluation of the intestines. This evaluation includes initial identification of structures, determination of their location, and systematic manual evaluation of all of the intestine the surgeon can reach. Often in cases of colic there is extensive gas and fluid accumulation in various areas of the intestine. To facilitate evaluation of the abdomen and intestines, the surgeon removes this gas and fluid with a needle attached to a suction device.

## MAKING DECISIONS DURING SURGERY

Because most colic surgeries are "exploratory" in their initial approach, a diagnosis is often only clear after the surgeons have completely evaluated the abdomen and intestines by their manual "search" of the abdomen. This process may at least be partially described as "running the bowel." It describes the process of manually locating a specific and anatomically constant location of the intestine and running a hand along the intestine in each direction (toward the stomach and toward the rectum) to the farthest normally reachable segment of intestine. Toward the stomach, the first segment of small intestine (the duodenum) is the usual stop-point. Toward the rectum, most of the large intestine can be followed to the small colon, the segment just before the rectum.

This highly regimented approach allows the surgeon(s) to identify abnormal-feeling intestinal segments, masses, entrapped areas of intestine, and physically blocked intestine, and to evaluate for appropriate location of intestine. Furthermore, the surgeon can evaluate much of the intestine by sight to help determine intestinal viability. Such assessment helps the surgeon determine whether a segment of intestine has suffered from occlusion of blood supply and damage from reduced oxygen delivery.

To describe more completely the abdominal exploratory surgery from a mechanical standpoint, you might think of reaching into a duffel bag that has a long piece of rope attached to both ends within the bag. The rope only fits inside when placed in a specific way. Not all of the rope is visible when you are looking into the bag; thus, much of the rope can only be felt because its attachments within the bag, the depth of the bag, and all of the top coils of the rope obscure the lower segments.

Once the surgeon has diagnosed the problem and assessed the intestinal health of the affected areas, the he will make some decisions. Depending on the diagnosis, these decisions may include whether the affected intestine is healthy enough to be left in the abdomen. If not, removal of the affected intestine can be performed (resection). Other possible decisions include determining whether an obstruction will require surgical extrication (by enterotomy), whether a mass or an area of thickened intestine should be biopsied, and whether a segment of the intestinal tract will require a surgical bypass by joining two segments that do not normally join anatomically (anastomosis). In addition, during surgery the surgeon also makes decisions based on the owner's wishes. For instance, a large piece of unhealthy intestine in a very unstable horse might pose a poor prognosis for survival. Because the diagnosis of the problem causing the colic and the condition and health of the intestine are not known until the surgeon can explore the abdomen, it is highly advisable for an owner or the owner's agent to be available during the surgery by phone. In this manner the surgeon is able to convey the overall findings of the surgery to the owner or agent with an explanation of the overall health of the affected intestine, the procedures required to correct the problem, the projected expenses for surgery and recovery, and the overall prognosis for recovery from surgery and for survival.

## RECOVERY FROM ANESTHESIA

Any time a horse undergoes general anesthesia, recovery is a major event because of the size and behavior of the horse coming out of the anesthesia. Nonetheless, recovery has come a long way, and horses benefit from the use of today's inhalant and injectable anesthetics and medications that help to minimize rough recoveries. Uncommonly, horses may suffer limb fractures or other significant trauma during recovery. Other potential complications in horses that have undergone general anesthesia include nerve paralysis of a limb (usually a forelimb) and significant muscle damage. Occasionally, horses, like some people, may respond poorly to the anesthesia and suffer organ damage due to an "allergic type" of response or from poor oxygen supply to an organ. Horses with hyperkalemic periodic paralysis (HYPP) or other muscle diseases such as polysaccharide storage myopathy (PSSM) are at increased risks of having muscle-related problems during recovery.

Most referral hospitals routinely use padded "recovery stalls" for both induction of and recovery from anesthesia. These stalls are specifically designed with protective padding for this purpose.

## POST-SURGICAL MANAGEMENT

Horses recovering from abdominal surgery will require post-operative care in some manner. Recovery and management can range from relatively simple to highly intensive. Factors that affect the complexity of post-surgical management include the overall health status of the horse as it entered surgery, the stability of the horse's health during and after the surgery, the procedure(s) required in surgery to correct the cause of the colic, the duration of the surgery, the specific cause of the colic (the diagnosis), the ability to correct the cause of the colic, and the ability of the intestinal tract to function normally afterward. Any of the above factors that contribute to making the horse sicker are likely to increase the need for more intensive post-operative therapy. For instance, horses that have high heart rates, copious amounts of reflux, abnormal abdominal fluid, and intractable pain are much more likely to require more extensive intensive care after surgery than a horse with mild colic pain, no reflux, and normal abdominal fluid. The overall health of a horse with colic may change rapidly from moment to moment. Horses that exhibit significant dehydration, low white cell counts, high heart rates, and poor organ perfusion will probably do less well in surgery and under general anesthesia. Some horses may go into surgery with relatively few indications of instability yet may become critical during or after surgery. Horses that are significantly unstable before or during surgery are at much higher risks of having significant problems related to anesthesia. Indeed, a horse may be so unstable or become unstable enough to die on the surgery table despite the most advanced efforts in emergency and critical care.

Certain surgical procedures also lend themselves to the need for more intensive post-operative care. Horses that require intestinal resections and anastamoses (removal of a segment of affected intestine and suturing of the remaining healthy ends back together) are likely to require significant intensive care after surgery. An enterotomy (opening the intestine itself to remove an obstruction) is another procedure that may increase the requirements for intensive care after surgery.

Horses that become endotoxemic are also likely to require more intensive post-operative care. Intestine recovering from the colic episode and surgery can take many days for its normal function to return. During this time some horses might become affected with endotoxemia (see Chapter 3, on endotoxemia). These horses will require additional intensive therapies to restore normal intestinal and cardiovascular function and to minimize complications often associated with endotoxemia.

Certain causes of colic lend themselves to the persistence of intestinal dysfunction and to the development of endotoxemia. Diarrhea, while often secondary to a primary intestinal dysfunction after colic surgery, often requires intensive therapy. Diarrhea may also be a primary problem due to various infectious agents such as bacteria and viruses. A horse with diarrhea due to any cause often requires intensive care. Although intestinal resections are highly associated with the need for intensive care after surgery, not all horses need it.

On occasion not all of the unhealthy intestine can be removed by resection. This is often due to the limitations imposed by the anatomy of the equine intestinal tract (inaccessible portions of affected intestine). Obviously, such horses are more likely to require additional post-operative treatment to return to physiologically satisfactory function. Some of these horses may never be able to recover.

## THERAPIES IN POST-OPERATIVE INTENSIVE CARE MANAGEMENT OF THE SURGICAL COLIC PATIENT

Many of the therapies used for post-surgical management have been described and discussed in the previous sections. Although their presentation was in the context of the evaluation and initial therapy for horses with colic due to unknown conditions, similar therapies are also employed after surgery when there is indication for their use. These same therapies are used because they function to restore stability to the patient and to assist in the return of normal intestinal function both before a diagnosis has been reached and after a medical or surgical correction has been completed. In a colic situation requiring surgical correction, these therapies alone will not restore normal intestinal function and only help stabilize the patient for a limited time. However, after surgical correction has been achieved, these therapies become important in helping to re-establish normal intestinal function and patient stability. Horses that have undergone colic surgery often require this extra management to recover fully. Because the intestinal tract often cannot immediately begin to function normally after surgery, intestinal motility is often reduced significantly.

Therapies to help stimulate the intestinal tract motility are often employed using some of the medications (prokinetic drugs) previously discussed, in addition to supplements in the intravenous fluids such as calcium and potassium. During this time it may be routinely necessary to remove fluid that accumulates in the stomach and small intestine (reflux) due to poor intestinal motility. This is particularly common when the primary cause of the colic involves the small intestine.

Another common post-operative therapy is antibiotic administration. This is important since the abdomen was opened with surgery, increasing the risks of the development of bacterial infection of the abdomen and/or the incision site. When an enterotomy is performed, antibiotic therapy after surgery is commonly prolonged because the abdomen has been exposed to the intestinal contents by the opening of the intestine itself, greatly increasing the risk of developing post-operative infections.

Intravenous fluid therapy is commonly provided to post-operative patients for several reasons: 1) horses may still tend to be dehydrated after colic surgery, 2) fluid therapy may support intestinal motility, 3) horses that have had abdominal surgery may be prohibited from eating and drinking for some time after surgery, necessitating intravenous fluids, and 4) intravenous fluids provide a vehicle for the administration of other medications and minerals that help promote intestinal healing and motility.

Other medications combat endotoxemia and the associated potential development of laminitis. These anti-endotoxic therapies are described in Chapter 3. In addition to these anti-endotoxic medications, drugs for post-operative pain management are also often necessary. Pain control may be achieved relatively easily with simple non-steroidal anti-inflammatory drugs such as flunixin meglumine (Banamine®), ketoprofen, phenylbutazone, etc. More intense post-operative pain will require more intensive intervention for pain management such as continuous infusion of butorphanol or other pain medications.

## POST-OPERATIVE COMPLICATIONS

Fortunately, serious post-operative complications are relatively uncommon. Anesthesia can cause complications, including nerve inflammation of a limb (neuritis), muscle inflammation and swelling (myositis), and development of post-operative central nervous system impairment (brain and/or spinal cord dysfunction). Neuritis of a nerve in a limb is probably one of the more commonly occurring post-operative complications. Supportive care and anti-inflammatory therapy are usually effective in helping the condition to resolve. A nerve that is commonly affected is the radial nerve in a forelimb. The result is the appearance of a "dropped elbow" and the inability to move the limb forward and to bear weight normally.

Muscle damage may also occur. It can be either localized in a certain body area or generalized over the entire muscle mass of the horse. Horses particularly at risk are those with primary muscle disorders such as hyperkalemic periodic paralysis and polysaccharide storage myopathy. Post-operative complications relating to the central nervous system are uncommon but can be related to the anesthetic agent or trauma from recovery. Limb fracture can occur in some horses during the recovery period. Death is always a possible complication to anesthetic administration. As explained earlier, many of these possible complications are related to the size of the animal and to idiosyncratic reactions to the anesthesia.

Other post-operative complications may be more directly related to surgery or to the procedures required for surgery. Post-operative incisional infections are not uncommon. These are managed by regular cleansing of the incision and antibiotic administration. Abdominal surgery of any type is always a risk factor for the development of septic peritonitis. Indeed, non-septic peritonitis is induced by the surgical incision itself. Septic peritonitis is associated with bacterial infection of the abdominal cavity and can occur with any abdominal surgery but is much more common when the intestine has been opened in any manner. Horses that develop bacterial infection of the abdominal cavity or have undergone small intestinal surgery may also be at increased risk of developing post-operative adhesions or bands of scar tissue attached to the intestine and areas of the abdominal cavity. Remarkably, this is not a highly common occurrence in adult horses. However, foals seem more prone to develop adhesions easily, even with uncomplicated intra-operative handling of the intestine (handling of the intestine during surgery). Adhesions in any horse are a problem because they can lead to the development of colic and can become a source of chronic, recurrent colic. Excess scarring of an anastomosis site can lead to a reduction in the lumen of the intestine (a stenosis). This can lead to other partial or complete obstructions, abnormal intestinal function and motility, and recurrent future colic. Other post-operative complications may include the development of laminitis, bacterial pneumonia and/or pleuritis, wound dehiscence (breaking open the stitches in the abdomen), venous thrombosis (clotting of blood in the veins), cardiac arrhythmias (abnormal heart rhythms), and kidney failure. Generally speaking, the "sicker" the horse is going into surgery and/or during surgery, the greater the risk for developing significant post-operative complications.

## RECOVERY FROM SURGERY

Horses do not recover rapidly from abdominal surgery. Opening of the abdomen of a large quadrupedal animal requires significant changes in routine for the animal for several months following the surgery. Without complications, an owner can expect the attending veterinarian(s) gradually to reintroduce feeding immediately after surgery. The volume of feed is reduced to compensate for a reduced activity level. In fact, many horses do very well receiving only high-quality hay once the surgeon has authorized feeding. Grain feeding may be altogether unnecessary and perhaps even discouraged. Strict stall confinement and hand walking are necessary in the immediate post-surgical period. This management causes minimal stress on the incision site, allowing the incision to heal safely and without concern of acute incisional breakdown and subsequent evisceration. For this reason exercise and free turnout are not good ideas. Recommendations for activity after abdominal surgery vary with the surgeon and the individual animal's rate of healing. However, minimal expectations probably include hand walking and stall rest for about one month, after which time the horse may be turned out in a small paddock for a few hours a day for another month. Regular turnout is often introduced at this time for another month, but some surgeons may permit gradual return to regular exercise without this third month. It generally takes at least two complete months or more for the horse to return to full, uninhibited exercise and training. This depends on the surgeon and the presence of post-surgical complications. As the activity level increases approaching this point, feed can gradually increase with it.

## CONCLUSION

Understanding and managing colic situations successfully requires good preventive health care and management on the part of the owner or caretakers, plans for handling emergency situations, and a good relationship with an equine veterinarian. Financial and time commitments should be seriously considered before you decide to own horses, as just providing good health care, housing, and nutrition can require extensive commitments, let alone those commitments required in colic and other emergency situations.

The overall likelihood of an individual horse requiring colic surgery is not great but is much higher in this species than most others. An owner should be fully prepared to handle the needs and decisions required in the instance of a surgical or medically intensive colic situation. Surgical and medically intensive interventions are often successful when the situations are handled appropriately with cooperation between the owner/caretakers and the attending veterinarian.

This book supplies a solid foundation for the layperson to

understand many of the important aspects of the causes and conditions of colic in the horse, their evaluation, and their management and treatments. However, you should realize that it is not possible to teach and explain all that is necessary to understand this huge topic within the confines of this book. Your veterinarian has received very complete training and experience in this area. Therefore, he/she should be the ultimate source for your guidance and recommendations in any area pertaining to your horse's well being. If your veterinarian chooses to evaluate, perform, or institute some other diagnostics, therapeutics, procedures, or managements that do not match what has been described in this book, you should realize that he/she is basing these decisions on his/her complete training and is the most informed individual in handling the specific situation that is present in your horse.

Do be proactive in your involvement with the understanding, prevention, management, and treatment of colic in your horses. This book will assist you in doing this successfully. However, your regular equine veterinarian should guide the ultimate recommendations and interventions on behalf of your horses.

# GLOSSARY

**Abdominocentesis** — Sampling of abdominal fluid by placement of a needle or a similar instrument into the abdominal cavity.

**Absorption tests** — Generally carbohydrates (glucose, lactose, or xylose) are administered at a specific dosage by nasogastric tube and blood samples are drawn in order to detect the subsequent blood levels at defined time intervals after the dosing of the carbohydrate. The results give an indication of the ability to absorb carbohydrate.

**Acetylcholine** — A stimulatory chemical in the intestinal nervous system that promotes intestinal motility. This chemical also exists elsewhere in the general nervous system where it has other effects.

**Acetylcysteine** — A drug that is used in veterinary medicine in order to help break down specific types of chemical bonds in protein.

**Acid/base disturbance** — A deviation of the body or organ pH from the normal 7.4.

**Acidosis** — A pH in the body or in the tissue that is lower than 7.35 (an acid pH).

**Adhesion** — A piece of scar tissue that may form between organs or related tissues.

**Albumin** — The main protein component of blood.

**Alpha-adrenergic agonists** — In the context of this book, these are agents that cause sedation and pain relief (analgesia); they include xylazine, detomidine, and romifidine.

**Amylase** — An enzyme that digests starch and other carbohydrates.

**Analgesia** — Pain relief.

**Anastomosis** — In the context of this book, the surgical joining of two ends of intestine, usually after a piece of intestine between these two ends has been removed.

**Antemortem** — Before death.

**Anterior enteritis** — Also known as duodenitis/proximal jejunitis, it is an inflammatory condition of the small intestine that produces large amounts of stomach reflux from a nasogastric tube, colic, and often depression and fever. It is usually handled without surgery but is difficult to differentiate from a small intestinal surgical problem.

**Anti-endotoxic effects** — Effects produced directly or indirectly by various medications that help combat endotoxemia or the effects of endotoxemia (such as SIRS — see Systemic Inflammatory Response Syndrome).

**Antiserum** — A blood product that contains antibodies against a specific agent. In the context of this book, often against endotoxin.

**Atrophy** — Reduction in size of an organ or tissue.

**Auscultation** — The act of listening with a stethoscope.

**Autonomic nervous system** — The part of the nervous system that functions without having to think about it (e.g., control of the heart rate, intestinal movements, sweating, etc.).

**Barium** — A commonly used contrast agent for taking X-rays that shows the outlines and shapes of the intestinal tract (necessary because this cannot be easily seen without the use of something that can be seen on X-rays while it fills the space inside the intestines).

**Bicarbonate** (buffer) — The compound that serves to neutralize acid production in the body.

**Bile duct** — The tube that exits from the bile tracts in the liver and connects to the small intestine (the duodenum).

**Biliary** — Refers to the bile tract, which extends from in the liver, through the common bile duct, to the opening into the duodenum.

**Biochemical dysfunction** — A dysfunction of the normal metabolic processes.

**Biopsy** — Surgical sampling of a piece of tissue.

**Blister beetles** — Beetles that are often found in alfalfa hay and that produce a poison called cantharidin, which produces the signs of blister beetle poisoning.

**Blood-brain barrier** — A theoretical barrier that exists between the blood and the tissue of the central nervous system that provides a barrier to many types of medications and blood proteins.

**Blood urea nitrogen** — In the context of this book, a blood parameter used to help identify kidney function.

**Borborygmi** — Intestinal sounds heard with a stethoscope or by ear.

**Broad ligament** — A ligament associated with the uterus and ovaries.

**Buffer** — To neutralize an acid or a base in the blood; or a compound that serves to perform this function (such as bicarbonate).

**Cantharidin** — The toxin produced by blister beetles.

**Capillary refill time** — The time required for the tissue of the gums to become pink again after blanching (turning white) under pressure of a finger. A clinical parameter to help evaluate tissue perfusion with blood.

**Carbohydrate** — A complex molecule of many sugars; broken down it produces sugar molecules.

**Cardiovascular** — Referring to the heart and the system of blood vessels.

**Catheter** — A piece of tubing (rigid tubing for venous catheters) that provides a portal for injecting medication and/or draining fluid. These can be venous catheters, arterial catheters, urinary catheters, and others.

**Cecocolic orifice** — The junction and communication of the cecum with the colon.

**Cecum** — A large blind-ended sac that serves as a location for fermentation in the horse. It is found at the very end of the small intestinal segment and at the very beginning of the large intestinal segment. It is considered to be part of the large intestine.

**Celiotomy** — Surgical incision and entry into the abdomen.

**Cellulose** — A structural carbohydrate in green plants that can be broken down by bacteria and protozoa in the large intestine of the horse. It produces absorbable forms of energy for the horse (volatile fatty acids).

**Choke** — Esophageal obstruction.

**Clotting profile** — A series of blood tests that evaluate all the pathways of blood clot formation.

**Coffin bone** — The bone in the hoof of the horse; also known as the third phalanx or P3.

**Colic** — Abdominal pain.

**Colitis** — Inflammation of the large intestinal tract that often produces diarrhea and/or protein loss.

**Colonic torsion** — A twisting of the large colon that may cause strangulation of the blood supply.

**Colloid** — The protein components of the blood.

**Complete blood count** (CBC) — A blood test that displays the relative amounts of red and white blood cells, the packed cell volume, and protein content of the blood.

**Computed tomography** — A "CAT scan"; a particular mode of imaging the body with very high detail.

**Contraindicated** — Against recommendations and possibly counterproductive in the process of diagnosis or treatment.

**Cranial nerve** — A nerve that is part of a set of 12 nerves that supply the head and neck for special senses, glands, and muscles.

**Creatinine** — A parameter of the serum biochemistry that helps to interpret kidney function. Creatinine is produced by muscle turn-over and it is cleared by the kidneys.

**Cribbing** — A vice displayed by some horses that involves grabbing objects with the teeth and swallowing air. Some horses may learn to swallow air without grabbing objects with the mouth.

**Cyathostomes** — Another name for the small strongyle group of intestinal parasites.

**Dehiscence** — Breakdown of a surgically closed wound.

**Diaphragmatic flexure** — The site where the left dorsal colon (that sits on top of the left ventral colon) courses toward the head from the back end of the horse and then behind the diaphragm, changes direction from the left side of the body to the right side of the body, giving rise to the right dorsal colon (that sits atop the right ventral colon).

**Dimethyl sulfoxide** (DMSO) — A chemical solvent that is used in veterinary medicine (particularly equine medicine) as a drug with anti-inflammatory properties.

**Dioctyl sodium sulfosuccinate** (DSS) — A drug that is administered by a nasogastric tube to horses. It serves to help break down impactions but can irritate the intestine.

**Diverticulum** — An outpouching (usually abnormal) that forms an enlarged space from a structure from which it develops (similar to overstretching and not being able to return to normal size).

**Dorsal** — Toward the spine of the horse.

**Duodenitis/proximal jejunitis** — The appropriate terminology for anterior enteritis (see Anterior enteritis).

**Duodenum** — The first segment of small intestine usually about 1 meter long (three feet).

**Dysphagia** — Inability to swallow normally.

**Dystocia** — Problems giving birth that result in inability to pass the foal through the birth canal.

**Edema** — Abnormal fluid accumulation in the tissues.

**Embryo** — The very earliest developmental stage of a foal in the uterus.

**Electrolytes** — The minerals and salts that exist in the blood and tissue fluids.

**Encyst** — Formation of a discrete and self-contained enclosure within a tissue.

**Endoscopy** — The examination of a patient with the use of an endoscope.

**Endotoxemia** — The presence of endotoxin within the circulation; this term is also often used to imply the presence of clinical signs that are associated with this endotoxin's presence in the circulation (see Systemic Inflammatory Response Syndrome — SIRS).

**Endotoxin** — The culprit in the development of systemic inflammatory response syndrome; it is literally part of gram-negative bacteria that is released by them when they die or replicate rapidly.

**Enteric nervous system** — The part of the nervous system that exists in the intestine and governs its movement and secretions.

**Enteritis** — Inflammation of the intestine; often implied to refer to the small intestine.

**Enterolith** — A stone that forms in the intestinal tract.

**Enterotomy** — Surgical incision into the intestinal tract from the outside of the intestine (approached from in the abdomen).

**Epidemiology** (epidemiologic) — The study of diseases and their occurrences at a population level.

**Epidural** — A space that overlies the spinal cord; often this term is used to refer to the procedure of placing a medication into this space for pain relief or for anesthesia (a nerve block) at the very end of the spinal cord (right at the head of the tail).

**Etiology** — The cause of.

**Evisceration** — The loss of abdominal contents through the abdominal wall, as through a surgical incision that has broken down.

**Fecalith** — An accretion or formation of a solid ball of fecal material.

**Fermentation** — The process by which bacteria in the large intestine of the horse break down the structural carbohydrate of plants such as cellulose and hemicellulose. The process thereby liberates energy from these carbohydrates that would otherwise not be able to be used by the horse.

**Fluoroscope** — An X-ray machine that provides real-time images; motion can be seen like in a video camera. This imaging technique is often used to look at intestinal movements with the aid of a contrast agent such as barium.

**Forage** — The grazing portion of the diet.

**Foramen** — A normal anatomical hole in any body structure.

**Founder** — A result of laminitis; the sinking or rotation of the coffin bone in the hoof of the horse.

**Frog** — The triangular-shaped "rubbery" tissue on the sole of a horse's foot that serves as a shock absorber.

**Ganglia** — An anatomical portion of the nervous system where there is a nest of nerve cell bodies.

**Gastrosplenic ligament** — A ligament that runs from the stomach to the spleen.

**General anesthesia** — Use of anesthetic agents to put the horse to sleep for surgery or other procedures.

**Glucose** — A simple sugar.

**Gram-negative** (bacteria) — A group of bacteria that is described by its lack of staining with gram stain.

**Hematology** — All-encompassing term that refers to the evaluation of blood cell counts and parameters.

**Hematoma** — A swelling that forms and is filled with blood.

**Hemicellulose** — A type of plant structural carbohydrate.

**Hemodynamic** — Referring to the effects on blood pressure and heart blood output.

**Hemoperitoneum** — Presence of blood in the abdomen.

**Herbivore** — An animal that is designed to eat plants.

**Hernia** — In the context of this book, the abnormal protrusion or slippage of intestine through a normal or an abnormal hole present in the abdomen.

**Hetastarch** — A synthetic fluid (colloid) that provides expansion of blood volume and is not lost into the tissues as readily as regular IV fluids (crystalloids).

**Hobbles** — In the context of this book, straps that are placed around pasterns to facilitate lifting of the horse by a hoist.

**Hoist** — A mechanical lift with a chain used to hoist the horse for surgery.

**Hyperlipemia** — The state of excess lipid (fat) in the horse's blood.

**Hypertonic saline** — Concentrated saline solution that serves to draw water into the blood vessels (volume expansion) by osmosis.

**Hypocalcemia** — The state of low blood calcium.

**Hypoproteinemia** — The state of low blood protein; usually because of protein loss.

**Icterus** — Yellow coloring of the mucous membranes; usually because of excess bilirubin in the blood.

**Ileocecal orifice** — The junction and communication of the cecum with the ileum (small intestine).

**Ileum** — The last segment of small intestine before reaching the cecum; usually about 1 meter (three feet) long.

**Ileus** — Reduced or non-progressive intestinal motility.

**Immune-mediated** — A condition that is mediated directly or indirectly by the response of the immune system.

**Impaction** — An accumulation of intestinal contents, often fecal material, that are unable to be easily passed.

**Infiltration** —In the context of this book, excess movement of cells into a tissue.

**Idiopathic** — Due to unknown cause.

**Infusion** (continuous) — A volume of medication or fluid that is injected into the blood by use of a venous catheter; continuous infusion is a continual flow of medication or fluid into the blood.

**Ingesta** — The intestinal contents.

**Intestinal motility** — Movement of intestine.

**Intramuscular** — Into the muscle.

**Intravenous** — Into the veins.

**Intussusception** — A segment of intestine "telescopes" into itself such that one piece slides into another adjacent segment.

**Intussusceptum** — The portion of an intussusception that slides into the adjacent segment.

**Intussuscipiens** — The portion of an intussusception that receives the intussusceptum.

**Iohexol** — A contrast agent (similar to barium) that is used outside of the intestinal tract or for a suspected leakage of the intestinal tract.

**Ischemia** — Lack of blood supply and associated tissue damage.

**J5 plasma** — Plasma harvested from hyperimmunized horses against endotoxin; therefore, concentrations of antibodies against endotoxin are high in this plasma.

**Jaundice** — Similar to the term icterus; yellow coloration to the mucous membranes.

**Jejunum** — The longest segment of small intestine that begins after the duodenum; usually about 20 meters in length.

**Lactate** — An acid that accumulates after anaerobic metabolism (metabolism without oxygen); this is the same thing as lactic acid.

**Lactose** — A sugar that may be used in some absorption tests.

**Laminitis** — Inflammation of the soft tissue attachment of the hoof to the coffin bone; severe cases may lead to founder.

**Laparoscopy** — Abdominal exploratory surgery through the use of a laparoscope, which allows only very small incisions to be made in the flank of the horse and allows the exploration of the abdomen to be performed in the standing (unanesthetized) horse.

**Large colon** — The portion of the large intestine that helps the cecum with fermentation and the absorption of water from the feces. It begins at the cecocolic orifice (from the cecum) and ends at the transverse colon. It is about 3 to 3.7 meters in length.

**Large intestine** — Everything other than small intestine and the rectum. Large intestine includes the cecum, the large colon, transverse colon, and the small colon.

**Larval** (larvae) — Referring to the infant stages of intestinal worms.

**Laxative** — Any medication that helps to increase movement of ingesta through the intestinal tract.

**Lignin** — A form of fiber in plants that cannot be digested by either the horse or the bacteria and protozoa in its intestinal tract.

**Lipase** — An enzyme that breaks down fat.

**Lipoma** — A benign fatty tumor often found in an older horse's abdomen.

**Lumen** — The inside space of the intestine or any other anatomical tube.

**Lymphosarcoma** — A cancerous disease of the lymphatic system.

**Lysis** — Breakdown or explosion.

**Macromolecule** — A complex molecule made up of many smaller molecules of a certain type.

**Magnetic resonance imaging** (MRI) — A diagnostic imaging technique that provides very high detail of soft tissue structures.

**Malabsorption** — Abnormally poor absorption.

**Maldigestion** — Abnormal digestion.

**Margo plicatus** — The line of the junction of the non-glandular mucosa (lining) of the stomach to the glandular mucosa.

**Mastication** — The act of chewing.

**Meckel's diverticulum** — A blind-ended extension from the surface of the jejunum or the ileum that is a remnant of the duct that connects the yolk of the embryo to the embryonic intestinal tract.

**Meconium** — The first, very thick and dark feces passed by a foal.

**Megaesophagus** — A condition that is associated with poor esophageal motility and enlargement of the internal size (the lumen) of the esophagus.

**Mesentery** — Ligamentous attachment of the intestine to the body wall of the horse.

**Mesodiverticular band** — A band of tissue that develops from the artery supplying the yolk sac of the embryo and its associated mesentery which fails to atrophy (as it should) during development.

**Microbiology** — The study of bacteria and viruses (microbes).

**Morphology** — Physical shape and composition.

**Mucosa** — In the context of this book, the inner lining of the intestinal tract that has within it glands for secretion of mucus, contains enzymes for digestion, and provides surface area for absorption of nutrients and water.

**Mucous membranes** — The tissues that line some anatomical orifices such as the mouth and vagina. They are generally pink in color due to their high blood supply.

**Myositis** — Inflammation of the muscles.

**Nasogastric intubation** — Placement of a plastic or other type of tube into the nasal passage and down through the esophagus into the stomach. Most often placed to check for or to remove excess fluid (reflux) from the stomach.

**Necrosis** — The process by which tissue dies, often due to poor blood supply.

**Necrotic** — An adjective used to describe dead tissue.

**Neoplasia** — Cancer.

**Nephrosplenic ligament** — The ligament that runs between the left kidney and the spleen.

**Nephrosplenic space** — The space between the spleen and the left kidney through which the nephrosplenic ligament courses.

**Neurotransmitter** — A substance released at nerve endings that provides a message at the next adjacent nerve cell for conduction or dampening (depending on the type of neurotransmitter) of a nerve impulse.

**Non-steroidal anti-inflammatory drugs** (NSAIDs) — Drugs that act as anti-inflammatory agents and usually as pain killers (analgesics). These include flunixin meglumine (Banamine®), Phenylbutazone, ketoprofen, meclofenamic acid (Arquel®), aspirin, and others.

**Non-surgical manipulation** — In the context of this book, these are manipulations that may be executed without any surgical incision in order to help correct a cause of a colic.

**Nuclear scintigraphy** — A diagnostic imaging modality that requires the administration of a radioactive isotope and subsequent "scan" of the area(s) of interest using a gamma camera.

**Omentum** — The main piece of abdominal mesentery in the horse.

**Opioid** — Drugs that are derivatives or analogs of opium.

**Osmotic** — Draws water into.

**Oxyglobin** — Purified bovine hemoglobin; used as a blood volume expander (colloid) that is capable of carrying oxygen as well.

**Packed cell volume** (PCV) — The percentage of the blood volume that is the red blood cell component. This tells you what the fluid portion of the blood is; since the packed cell volume is the "solid portion" or "cellular portion" the remainder is grossly the fluid portion. This parameter indirectly gives an appreciation for the amount of hydration or dehydration in the horse.

**Palliative** — Treating and managing only the clinical signs (as opposed to correcting the underlying problem).

**Pancreatic duct** — The tube that exits from the pancreas and ends in the duodenum, bringing pancreatic enzymes and other products necessary for digestion in the small intestine.

**Parietal** — Referring to the body wall of the abdominal cavity.

**Pathologist** — A specialist in evaluating tissues grossly and microscopically.

**Pelvic flexure** — The location in the large colon where the left ventral colon that is coursing toward the tail of the horse (from the sternal flexure) turns upward toward the spine and heads back toward the head of the horse as the left dorsal colon.

**Pepsin** — An enzyme that digests proteins.

**Percussion** — In the context of this book, a tapping or flicking of a finger against the body in order to evaluate the tone produced as evidence of a gas- or fluid-filled area of intestine.

**Perfusion** — The blood supply to an organ or tissue.

**Peritonitis** — Inflammation of the abdominal cavity (may be septic or non-septic).

**Phenylephrine** — In the context of this book, a drug that is used to cause contraction of the spleen in association with the non-surgical manipulation attempts to correct a nephrosplenic entrapment (left dorsal displacement of the colon).

**Physiology** — The biological processes that are necessary for the maintenance of normal function of the tissues, organs, and animal as a whole.

**Pica** — Deliberate consumption of non-food items; often used to describe deliberate ingestion of fecal material.

**Plasma** — The fluid portion of the blood that is high in protein.

**Pleuritis** — Inflammation of the chest cavity (may be septic or non-septic).

**Pleurodynia** — Pain in the chest cavity, most often associated with inflammation of the chest cavity (pleuritis).

**Polymixin B** — An aminoglycoside antibiotic that exhibits properties that help neutralize endotoxin in the blood.

**Pre-cecal segment** — The entire segment of intestine that precedes the cecum (mouth, esophagus, stomach, and small intestine).

**Prokinetic** — A drug that stimulates intestinal motility.

**Protozoa** — A group of non-bacterial unicellular microscopic organisms.

**Proximal** — In the context of this book, meaning closer to the mouth.

**Pseudo-obstruction** — Physiological dysfunction of the intestine that causes loss of progressive motility and subsequent backing up of intestinal contents.

**Psyllium hydrophilic mucilloid** (Metamucil®) — A bulk laxative and also believed by some to be helpful in removing sand from the intestinal tract of the horse.

**Pylorus** — The last portion of the stomach before the duodenum (small intestine), equipped with a muscular sphincter.

**Radiography** — Diagnostic imaging technique using conventional X-rays with or without contrast agents such as barium.

**Recumbency** — Lying down or unable to rise.

**Rectal tear** — Traumatic disruption of the wall of the rectum most often secondary to a rectal examination. Four grades of rectal tears exist (see Chapter 3, Rectal Tears).

**Reflux** — Excess fluid accumulation in the stomach that subsequently spills out of the nose when pressures become high enough to cause this spontaneously or the excess fluid (reflux) can be removed by a nasogastric tube.

**Regurgitate** — Active process of vomiting.

**Resection** — In the context of this book, surgical removal of a diseased area of intestine.

**Right dorsal colitis** — A syndrome of colonic inflammation often associated with poor appetite, low protein, and intermittent colic. Most often associated with administration of non-steroidal anti-inflammatory drugs for long periods of time and/or in excessively high doses.

**Root of the mesentery** — The attachment of the mesentery to the body wall; also associated with the cranial mesenteric artery in the abdomen of the horse.

**Rupture** — In the context of this book, disruption of the integrity of the intestine anywhere along its length that leads to bacterial contamination of the surrounding cavity and/or tissues.

**Sand sounds** — Characteristic sounds heard most often just behind the sternum of the horse that are highly indicative of sand in the large intestine.

**Sedative** — Any drug that sedates.

**Sepsis** — The state of bacterial infection of any tissue or organ.

**Septic** — Often used as a description of the clinical condition associated with endotoxemia (like systemic inflammatory response syndrome); or a description of the presence of sepsis or bacterial contamination/infection.

**Serosa** — The outermost surface of intestine that is exposed to the abdominal cavity.

**Serum biochemistry** — A "catch all" panel of blood tests usually run together that evaluate organ function, cellular damage of organs, and electrolyte and protein levels in the blood.

**Shock** — The status of poor tissue perfusion and acidosis as a result of either poor blood volume for circulation (hemodynamic shock) or as a result of the effects of endotoxin on the body (septic shock).

**Skin tenting** — A highly subjective assessment of hydration in the horse using the length of time the skin stands up when pulled upward on the neck or shoulder.

**Small colon** — The segment of intestine between the transverse colon and the rectum where water is absorbed from the intestine to form fecal balls for excretion.

**Sodium bicarbonate** — A compound that is given by intravenous administration to help correct pH imbalances that have led to acidosis (in order to buffer the excess acid in the horse).

**Somatic nervous system** — The part of the general nervous system that controls the muscles that are under voluntary control (principally skeletal muscle).

**Spasmodic colic** — Colic allegedly caused by non-progressive spastic motility.

**Spasmolytic** — Drugs that act to cease spastic intestinal motility.

**Sphincter** — A muscular valve that exists between two segments of intestinal tract and that controls the rate of entrance of ingesta to the second segment. A sphincter also exists at the anus.

**Squamous** — The non-glandular portion of stomach that is lined with squamous cells along the surface of the inside of that portion of the stomach.

**Stasis** — Refers to the slowing or stoppage of intestinal motility.

**Stenosis** — Narrowing of the intestinal tract (including the esophagus) caused by external compression of the tract or by stricture (scarring) that leads to a narrowing of the lumen.

**Sternal flexure** — Location where the right ventral colon running on the right side of the abdomen toward the head turns to the left and gives rise to the left ventral colon running toward the tail of the horse and the pelvic flexure.

**Strangles** — A disease characterized by extensive abscessation of the lymph nodes of the head and caused by the bacterium *Streptococcus equi* spp. *equi.*

**Stricture** — A type of stenosis or narrowing of the lumen of any segment of the intestinal tract that is generally caused by excessive scarring.

**Synchronous diaphragmatic flutter** — A syndrome in which low blood calcium and often magnesium lead to a hyper-excitable state in the nerve that runs over the heart to control contraction of the diaphragm (the phrenic nerve). In this state, because the nerve fires very easily every time the heart produces electrical activity of contraction, it causes the phrenic nerve to fire and produce simultaneous contraction of the heart and the diaphragm (also known as "thumps").

**Symbiotic** — A parasitic relationship in which both the parasite and the host benefit from the relationship.

**Systemic Inflammatory Response Syndrome** (SIRS) — The clinical syndrome caused in response to endotoxemia that leads to poor tissue perfusion, ischemia, acidosis, and possibly to hemodynamic and septic shock.

**Tail of the spleen** — The blunt end of the spleen that can be felt by rectal palpation in the left side of the horse's abdomen.

**Theiler's disease** — Acute severe liver failure secondary to the administration of any products that are derived from equine blood or serum.

**Third phalanx** — The bone in the hoof of the horse, also called the coffin bone or pedal bone.

**Thromboembolism** — The access of a clot into the general circulation where it may lodge and lead to ischemia of any tissues supplied by the vessel(s) that it has clogged.

**Thumps** — A "lay" term for synchronous diaphragmatic flutter (see Synchronous diaphragmatic flutter).

**Transverse colon** — The segment of intestine immediately following the large colon and leading into the small colon.

**Trocharization** — Placement of a long needle or catheter through the body wall into gas-distended large intestine in order to relieve pressure.

**Ultrasonography** — A diagnostic imaging modality using transfer and reverberation of sound waves to produce an image.

**Uterine torsion** — Twisting of the uterus along the axis head to tail axis.

**Vascular** — Referring to the blood vessels.

**Ventral** — Toward the bottom of the abdomen of the horse.

**Ventral band of the cecum** — A large intestinal band that is used as a major landmark for identification of the cecum during rectal palpation.

**Vestigial** — Referring to a structure that has either no function or reduced function. Usually implies that this reduced function has come about with the evolution of the animal and with the structure within that animal.

**Viable** — Exhibits life; in the context of this book, viable intestine is judged by a surgeon in order to decide whether a segment must be removed. Viability is at least partially associated with adequate blood perfusion and color.

**Visceral** — Referring to the organs within the chest and abdominal cavity.

**Viscus** — A segment of intestine.

**Volatile fatty acids** — Acetate, butyrate, and propionate. These are the products of large intestinal fermentation of plant fibers that the horse's enzymes cannot digest. The bacteria that ferment these structural plant carbohydrates produce these compounds as absorbable and usable energy sources for the horse.

**Volvulus** — A twist of intestine.

**Vaporizer** —Equipment in the anesthesia machine that allows proper mixing of oxygen, air, and inhaled anesthetic agent in the correct concentrations to produce general anesthesia.

**Vascular space** — The volume of the blood vessels; changes with loss of body fluid (dehydration) and bleeding.

**Xylose** — A sugar used in some carbohydrate absorption tests.

## RECOMMENDED READINGS

Auer, JA, Stick, JA (ed). *Equine Surgery.* 2nd edition. Philadelphia: WB Saunders Company, 1999.

Mair, T, Divers, T, Ducharme, N (ed). *Manual of Equine Gastroenterology.* Philadelphia: WB Saunders, 2002.

*Nutritional Research for the Health of the Horse.* St. Louis, MO: Purina Mills Equine Nutritional Educational Programs, 2003.

Smith, BP (ed). *Large Animal Internal Medicine.* 2nd edition. St Louis, MO: Mosby, 1996.

*The Glass Horse* (Compact Disc). The University of Georgia, 2001. www.3Dglasshorse.com.

## Picture Credits

INTRODUCTION
Robin Peterson, 7.

CHAPTER ONE
Michael Ball, DVM, 26; Anne M. Eberhardt, 27.

CHAPTER TWO
Lee Thomas, 32; Anne M. Eberhardt, 35, 42, 46.

CHAPTER THREE
N. White, DVM, 60; Anne M. Eberhardt, 84.

CHAPTER FOUR
Anne M. Eberhardt, 129-133, 135, 136; Lee Thomas, 130; Bradford G. Bentz, VMD, 130, 134, 135.

COVER PHOTOGRAPH — LEE THOMAS

# About the Author

Bradford G. Bentz, VMD, MS, is a graduate of the University of Pennsylvania School of Veterinary Medicine. He received a master's degree in veterinary sciences at the University of Kentucky Maxwell H. Gluck Equine Research Center.

Bentz, who was born in Germany, is a Diplomate in Large

**Bradford G. Bentz**

Animal Internal Medicine with the American College of Veterinary Internal Medicine. He is certified in equine practice by the American Board of Veterinary Practitioners.

Bentz is an assistant professor in equine internal medicine at Oklahoma State University's College of Veterinary Medicine. He also maintains a private show horse practice.

Bentz has held numerous training and teaching positions and has served as a commission veterinarian for the Kentucky Racing Commission. He has prepared numerous papers for veterinary journals and has written for *The Horse: Your Guide to Equine Health Care*. He is the author of *Understanding Equine Neurological Disorders* and *Understanding Equine Preventive Medicine*, both published by Eclipse Press.

Bentz lives in Stillwater, Okla., with his wife, Patricia, and their son, Ian.